NEW YORK

# A Pictorial History

# NEW YORK

## MARSHALL B. DAVIDSON

CHARLES SCRIBNER'S SONS

*New York*

Library of Congress Cataloging in Publication Data

Davidson, Marshall B
   New York: A Pictorial History

   Bibliography
   Includes index.
   1. New York (State)—History—Pictorial works.
I. Title.
F120.D38         974.7'0022'2         77-3921

ISBN 0-684-14772-6

Title Page
New York skyscrapers around the turn of the century
Charles Scribner's Sons Art Files

Editor   NORMAN KOTKER

Assistant Editor   PATRICIA LUCA

Art Director   RONALD FARBER

# Contents

# *This Book and Its Uses*

One picture, as the saying has it, is worth a thousand words. If that is true, then this book, with its 750 or so pictures, illustrating innumerable aspects of New York life from the seventeenth century to the present, is equivalent to a massive volume on the history of the state, a volume much more comprehensive than any available at present. The aim of this book is to make the folk saying valid, to provide authoritative and thorough documentation of the rich and varied pictorial material that has evolved in the centuries of New York history and, by the inclusion of an extensive and unique index, to enable the reader and the reference librarian to find in the pictures themselves hundreds of facts which are unavailable elsewhere, or, if available, very difficult of access.

In this work, as in Scribner's notable *Album of American History,* which has proven so useful as a book of historical reference, the pictures themselves contain the history, and the text assumes a subordinate role. The captions aim merely to identify the pictures within a historical context, without intending to be in any sense a complete, however brief, narrative history of the state. In this book, we have a thread of text which explains the pictures, instead of scattered pictures which only scantily illustrate a text.

The plan of the book has been to reproduce only pictures which are contemporary with the events they illustrate. As a result, each picture is a primary source of historical information, a rich repository of facts about the period in which it was made. Most of us are not accustomed to looking at pictures in this way. We generally look at them aesthetically and as illustrations of a story, scene, or event, rather than as aggregates of historical facts. This book is designed to alter that balance, to enable the reader to "milk" the pictures, as it were, of the historical or factual information they contain, and to provide, through a comprehensive index, an instrument of reference and research.

An example will show the system by which this is done. The view of Utica, reproduced overleaf and on pages 160 and 161, is a lithograph showing the town around 1850. It is a fine example of a panoramic view of an American city, one of many which were produced in the nineteenth century. By consulting the index entry for the picture, under "Utica," and other appropriate entries, the reader can learn that the picture shows the following facts:

1. By 1850 treatment of the insane had progressed, for there was a fine asylum.
2. Utica was sizable enough to support three large hotels.
3. The town was served by the Utica and Syracuse Railroad.
4. Outside the railroad station, passenger coaches customarily waited to meet the train, as did freight wagons waiting for delivery of freight.
5. Pedestrian crosswalks were provided on the streets.

Not all these facts are in the caption, and some may not be readily apparent to the reader. The comprehensive index, which indicates the subjects which are illustrated but not discussed in the captions, is designed to provide these facts, to supply a key to each of the hundreds of pictures in the book. The index entries give the reader and researcher ready access to visual information that contains answers to a multitude of questions.

A typical entry will read:

stagecoach, c.1850, meeting train, 160–61:2 (left foreground)

The entry contains a picture number (2) as well as page numbers (160–61), indicating that the object is illustrated but not discussed in the caption. The year in which the object was made (c.1850) is indicated. Further information about it is provided for the reader. Some indication of its location in the picture is given. And finally, the page on which the subject appears and the picture number are given. Anyone interested in learning about the subject will find an informative illustration which is incorporated within an illustration of an entirely different subject. Thus, a book designed to document pictorially the history of one state—one volume in a series devoted to the pictorial history of all the states—has broader application, becoming, in effect, a distinguished pictorial reference library, encompassing numerous aspects of the varied life of America.

This view of Utica is cross-indexed under the following entries:

architecture, Greek Revival (station at lower left)
asylum, insane
pedestrian crosswalks
railroad boxcars
railroads
railroad stations
scaffolding, for awnings
stagecoaches, meeting train
Utica, New York:
    churches
    hotels
    New York State Asylum for the Insane
    railroad station
    stagecoach to
    streets
    views of
Utica and Syracuse railroad
wagon, freight, meeting train
wagon, lumber

Since the book contains other illustrations showing railroad stations and trains, hotels, lumber hauling, etc., elsewhere, the index will lead the reader to a wide range of information on the subject of his interest throughout the centuries of New York history.

This book is part of a series of volumes on the American states. The series will bring together an unequaled library of pictures devoted to American history, some 35,000 pictures in all, each different and each contemporary with the events described, ensuring its trustworthiness as a historical document. Eventually, a comprehensive index will be published for the entire series, providing on a national scale the same sort of reference documentation contained in individual volumes.

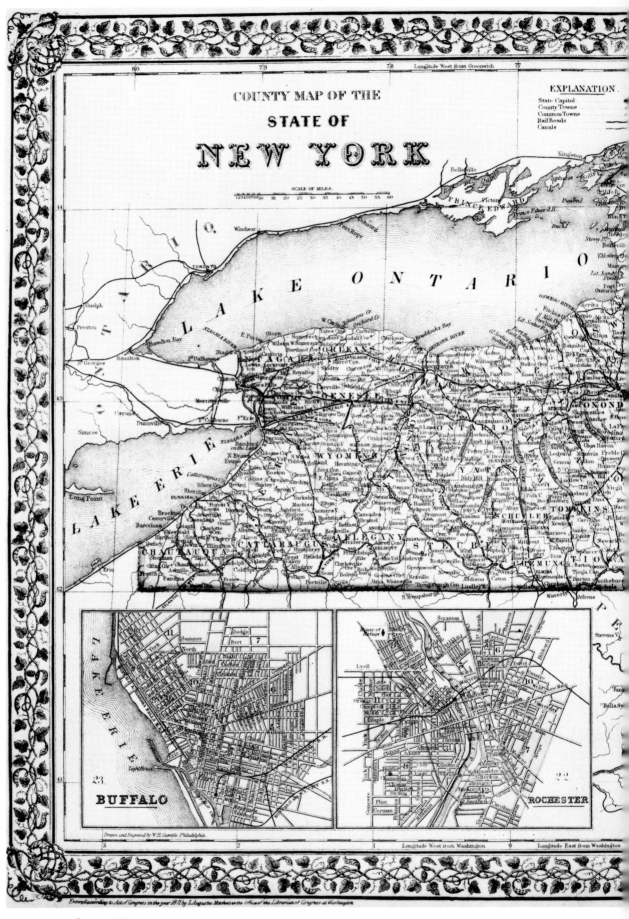

*New York—1871*

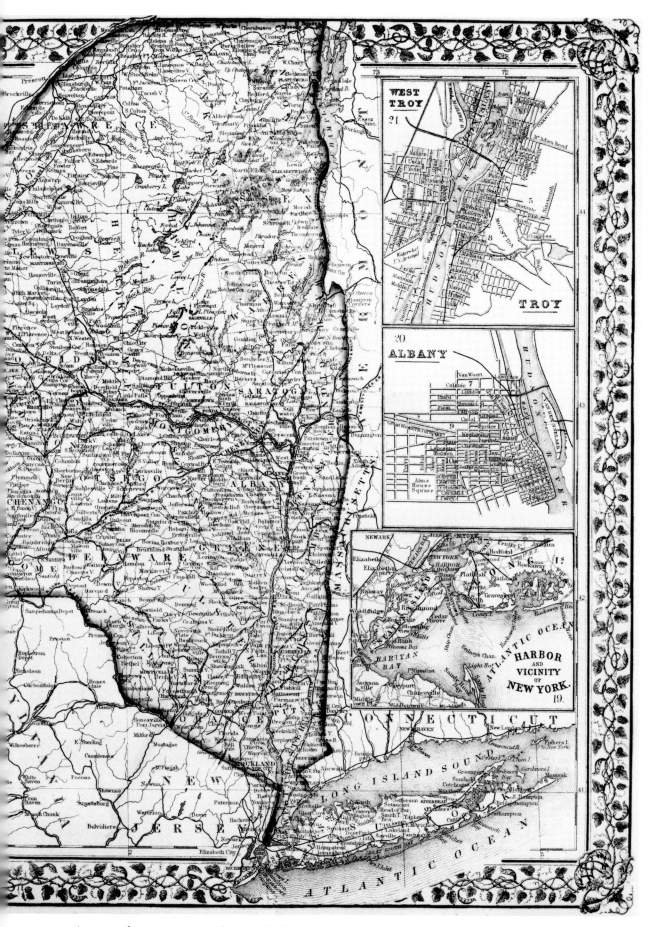

A county-by-county map of New York resembles a horn of plenty thrust down towards the sea from the north and west. OVERLEAF: Manhattan and Brooklyn.

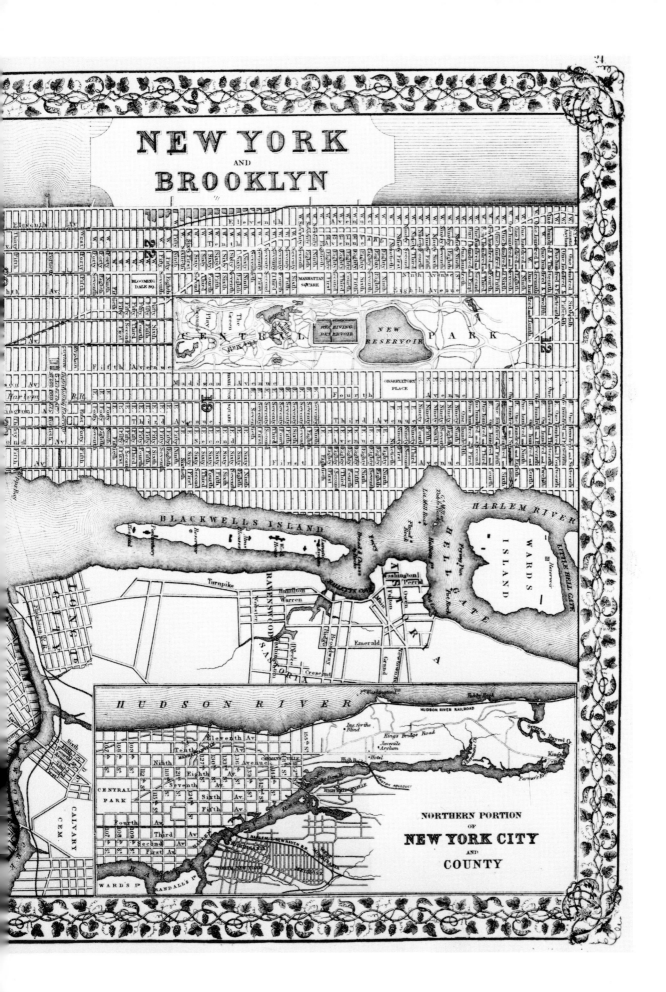

# NEW YORK
### AND
# BROOKLYN

NORTHERN PORTION
OF
**NEW YORK CITY**
AND
**COUNTY**

NEW YORK

# Introduction

From high in the air most of the land that comprises the state of New York looks puckered into hills and mountains, and laced by waterways that seek their outlets in all directions through innumerable valleys. In the northernmost corner the Adirondack Mountains, a spur of the Canadian highlands, jut across the international border to provide the state's most picturesque peaks. The tallest of those is barely a mile high, hardly comparable to the towering heights of the western ranges of the country. But the Adirondacks are ancient mountains, shaped of rocks that took their place above the primordial sea scores of millions of years before the Rockies were formed, rocks that are as old as any in the world known to geologists. Near the highest reaches of the forested uplands, from "a minute, unpretending tear of the clouds—a lovely pool shivering in the breeze of the mountains," spill the thin beginnings of the Hudson River, one of the world's most enchanting waterways.

Another province of mountains covers almost the entire southern portion of the state, rising in the Catskills to occasional relatively lofty summits overlooking the Hudson, and leveling off into a plateau that rolls gently southward into New Jersey and Pennsylvania and extends to the Great Lakes bordering the state on the west. They are products of hundreds of millions of years of erosion that has softened their contours and deepened their valleys. In one of those ample folds the water of the Schoharie Reservoir now covers the remains of the oldest forests known in the world, gigantic petrified stumps of fern trees, eleven feet in circumference, that flourished in the western Catskills far back toward the beginning of time.

Most of the long, straight eastern border of New York is edged by still different mountains, the Taconics, which geologists tell us are but worn stumps of a formation that must once have been of Alpine proportions. They are properly a margin of the New England geological province, but they are a welcome intrusion into the state, for they complete the master mold in which the destiny of New York was cast long before it was peopled by red men or white. The two broad valleys, the Hudson and the Mohawk, that cut at right angles between the separate highlands, provide a sweeping throughway from the Atlantic Ocean to the Great Lakes, the only water-level route through the coastal mountains which, from Georgia in the south to the St. Lawrence River in the north, block off the interior mass of the continent from the Atlantic. In time those cross-country valleys came to serve as the most heavily traveled migration route in history, channeling millions and more millions of expectant wanderers from the outside world toward the limitless new lands of the West. Compared with that epic movement of humanity, the barbarian invasions of the Roman Empire were, numerically, a minor affair and, it could be argued, hardly of greater consequence.

Over the years, that incessant stream of immigration has laid down a rich human deposit as it flowed through the land. About three quarters of the state's population is clustered along that historic route (as are most of its major cities), and more than half of those people are either immigrants themselves or of immigrant parentage. The character of New York, its culture, its social textures, and its daily life, has been significantly shaped—both richly benefited and hard-tried—by the need to accommodate the throngs that have settled within its borders. On a larger scale than any other state, New York has known the continuous ferment and restless excitement that attend the fusion of different peoples uprooted from their several soils and ancestries and cast together as in a crucible.

In area New York is not large as the states of America measure, ranking only thirtieth among the fifty. But within its relatively modest bounds the land has accommodated a wealth of human experience out of all proportion to its size. It has been a coveted land, for it promised abundance and authority to those who could invest and command it, and it long played an important and often bloody role in the strategy of nations.

Long before the white man came to settle in America, Indians found what was to become New York an ideal habitat. The wooded lands teemed with wild game and provided an abundance of fruit and nuts; fertile clearings produced corn, beans, and tobacco; the earth yielded edible roots and salt in ample quantities; streams and lakes swarmed with fish, and provided a communications network that reached to all points of the compass. There is reason to believe the ancient Indian legend that the Great Spirit regarded this land with special favor. The imprint of the hand he once laid upon it in benediction can still be traced in the tapered outlines of the Finger Lakes.

It is almost within the span of those clear-watered valleys, according to the Indian story, that Hiawatha dreamed and spoke of a peaceful brotherhood of man. And round about, covering practically all the present state from Lake Erie to the Hudson River, the tribes of the Iroquois in the sixteenth century did actually establish the league of the Five Nations (Mohawk, Oneida, Onondaga, Cayuga, and Seneca), a remarkably statesmanlike and democratic confederation of aboriginal tribes that for a time was the most powerful combination of Indians on the North American continent. In consolidating their position as virtual masters of the New York and adjoining areas, the Iroquois proved fearsome adversaries whose name struck terror among other tribes as far west as the Mississippi. Nevertheless, Hiawatha's concept of a lasting settlement in which all nations would sit down under the Tree of Peace was cherished in principle even when it was violated in fact. It has often been observed that such an ideal of democratic participation in a confederation of equal states may have influenced the white men when, at the birth of the United States of America, they framed first the Articles of Confederation and then the Constitution.

The Iroquois' first head-on confrontation with white men was a tragic event, with long-drawn-out, dire consequences. In 1609, prodding southward from his recently established base in Quebec, accompanied by a band of northern Indians, the French explorer Samuel de Champlain gave battle to a party of Iroquois who contested his way. With the first shot of his arquebus, loaded with four bullets, Champlain relates, he killed two Indians and mortally wounded a third. When one of his two French companions fired another shot from the surrounding woods, the astonished Iroquois, "seeing their chief dead . . . lost courage and took flight, abandoning their field and their fort, and fleeing into the depths of the forest." With that one paltry battle the French won the fierce, lasting enmity of the Five Nations. Had Champlain managed to find a peaceful way to the mouth of the Hudson River, he could have reached it before Henry Hudson and established the claims of France before the Dutch gained a foothold. In consequence the history of all North America might have been quite different. As it was, the Iroquois neither forgot nor forgave that first shot fired in their wilderness domain. Their enmity was long to be feared, their alliance to be coveted; their hireling tomahawks might strike death in any direction. And for most of the next two centuries they held the balance of power among the European nations and colonists contending for the mastery of America.

As the map of New York was gradually outlined (the final boundaries were not settled until 1880–81, when an Act of Congress ended a long dispute with Connecticut), it looked like a horn of plenty thrust down towards the sea from the north and west to receive the wealth of the continent and funnel it to the extreme limit of the land at Manhattan Island. Thus the English viewed it when they quietly and firmly took over Holland's claim in 1664. And thus also did the French, who for a century and a half held a counterclaim to the largest part of the present state, as the names of its counties and towns— St. Lawrence, Orleans, Montcalm, Chateaugay, and Raquette—continue to remind us.

Other place names, in the eastern part of the state—Brooklyn, Kinderhook, Cobleskill, Spuyten

Duyvil, and the like—recall Holland's relatively brief occupancy of those areas (as do such words as *cruller* and *cookie, boss* and *scow, stoop* and *dope,* which long ago found a fixed place in everyday American speech). The Dutch started to people the Hudson River valley following the pioneering visit of Henry Hudson who, a few months after Champlain's unfortunate skirmish with the Iroquois, in the late summer of 1609, sailed his little *Half Moon* as far as the present site of Albany. Hudson, an Englishman in the employ of the Dutch East India Company, was seeking a northwest passage to the Orient. Instead he discovered a rich lode of precious furs —of mink, beaver, and other pelts—that forester Indians would exchange in quantity for cheap trinkets. For the next century that lucrative fur trade gave shape to both the promises and the problems that New York offered the Europeans who ventured there. The Indians, principally the Iroquois, controlled the supply of furs, becoming ever more deeply involved in the contentious rivalry of the whites and with one another for shares in the spoils.

Through its trading company the Dutch tried to run their North American colony—New Netherlands, as it was called—as a business proposition. In 1624 eighteen French-speaking, Protestant, Walloon families settled at Fort Orange, which would become in time the capital city of Albany. A year later forty Dutch colonists landed at the tip of Manhattan Island, a spot which would in its turn become the wealthiest small area in the world, although it rose to little importance under Dutch rule. From the beginning, New Amsterdam, as the little settlement was named, was a sailors' town and, according to one witness, it soon acquired the arrogance and the sounds of Babel. As early as 1643 a visiting missionary overheard in and about its short streets the babble of eighteen different languages. "Our chief unhappyness here," complained one resident, "is too great a mixture" of different races and religions, an observation which has often been repeated in the last three hundred years.

For various good reasons westering English colonists were attracted to the Dutch territory in sizable numbers. "Doe not forbeare to . . . crowd on," the governor of neighboring Connecticut was instructed in 1642, "crowding the Dutch out of those places where they have occupied, but without hostility or any act of violence." So it

was that in 1664, when a small English fleet arrived to take over the colony, there were numerous Englishmen already in New Amsterdam to see it turned over to British rule "without a blow or a tear." Furious as he was over the usurpation, with no support from Holland, Governor Peter Stuyvesant could do nothing about it.

The takeover had been engineered by the Duke of York and Albany, brother of Charles II and later king himself, as James II. He had enjoined his governor, Richard Nicolls, to treat the Dutch with "humanity and gentleness." He made no effort to impose the English language or his Catholic religion on his new subjects. As a consequence, Dutch customs as well as the Dutch language persisted along the Hudson Valley until well into the last century.

However, the duke also made no effort to summon an assembly, and there were enough Englishmen already in the colony to cause him trouble when he chose to tax them without their representatives' consent. A code of laws similar to those of New England was drawn up by representatives of Long Island and Westchester, granting New Yorkers (as the inhabitants would now be termed) trial by jury, freedom of religion, and protection of property rights; it also authorized strong local governments with elected members. But that was not enough. In 1683 a "Charter of Liberties and Privileges" provided for an elective assembly and a Bill of Rights and reaffirmed religious freedom and trial by jury. However, that charter was repudiated by James on his accession to the throne of England two years later. When in turn he was dethroned, in the Glorious Revolution of 1688, New York broke out in a revolution of its own, led by the German-born merchant Jacob Leisler, in favor of a more popular government than had yet been secured. With another turn of the wheel Leisler was deposed and hanged for treason. But the principles for which he stood did not die with him. The rebellion he fostered widened a rift between the prominent and wealthy colonists on the one side and the small farmers, mechanics, and merchants on the other. Partly as a consequence of the issues that were raised, the aristocrats themselves divided into rival liberal and conservative factions. From this discord political parties were formed, each gathering to its cause diverse elements of the population. Eventually many of the reforms for which Leisler had died were hammered out in a practical manner.

Throughout the English colonial period the affairs of New York were dominated by what was virtually a feudal aristocracy. To encourage colonization the Dutch had offered free and sizable grants of land in the Hudson Valley to those individuals who would settle fifty families on any stated tract. The English confirmed the ownership of those large estates—patroonships, as they were called—and some royal governors made similar extravagant handouts to other favored individuals. One early governor complained that upon his accession the whole province had already been "given away to thirty persons." About a half century later, in 1764, Governor Cadwallader Colden wrote that three estates alone contained "above a million acres each, several others above 200,000," most of which still remained uncultivated, "without any benefit to the community." The manorial lords controlled not only most of the land, but also the politics, the law, the church, and—through intermarriage with prominent merchant families—the trade of the colony. The Livingstons, Schuylers, Rensselaers, Philipses, and other often-related families overawed not only the common folk but the royal governors to boot.

The monopolization of such vast areas of desirable land by a relatively few owners had an enduring effect on the development of New York. Together with the mountain barriers of the Catskills and the Adirondacks and threats from the French and Indians along the borderlands, it long discouraged any such substantial immigration as rapidly populated the hinterland of Pennsylvania in the eighteenth century. On the eve of the Revolution, after more than a century and a half of colonization, most of the New York countryside remained a wilderness. Only a scattering of settlers had moved more than a few miles from the coastal area and the Hudson and Mohawk rivers.

In spite of its relatively small and restricted population, New York remained the American key to the struggle for empire that was bringing England and France into confrontation on a global scale. Each of those nations coveted the routes that led most directly through New York to the heartland of North America; each looked to the Indians for support in their conflicting interests. In 1687, to placate and flatter the Five Nations, James II authorized the protection of these tribesmen as subjects of his realm. Proud of their new sovereignty, the Iroquois launched vigorous raids on French settlements along the St. Lawrence. That provoked retaliating raids by French and Indian war parties dispatched by the military governor of Canada, the comte de Frontenac. In 1690, without warning, the upstate town of Schenectady was destroyed and its inhabitants mercilessly butchered.

That was but a prelude to the strife the colony would suffer over the next several generations. Immediate fears were felt for the safety of Albany, major crossroads of the traffic in furs. "Albany is the dam," it was reported from Massachusetts, "which should it through neglect be broken down by the might of the Enemy, we dread to think of the Inundation of Calamities that would quickly follow thereupon." Albany did not fall, but those fears persisted. A half century later Benjamin Franklin, not usually an alarmist, warned his countrymen in lurid words of their peril from French and Indian attacks. "On the first alarm," he wrote, "terror will spread over all; and, as no man can with certainty know that another will stand by him, beyond doubt very many will seek safety by a speedy flight. . . . Sacking the city will be the first, and burning it, in all probability, the last act of the enemy. This, I believe, will be the case, if you have timely notice. But what must be your conditions, if suddenly surprised, without previous alarm, perhaps in the night!" In 1754 at a congress held at Albany, he called for a necessary union among the colonies that would plan concerted action in the defense of their borders.

Although nothing came of that proposal, the British home government, with William Pitt as prime minister, was concerned enough by a series of humiliating defeats at the hands of the French at such vital posts as Oswego and Ticonderoga to undertake vigorous offensive action. British victories in and around New York soon led to the ultimate victory of that campaign when Quebec fell to General Wolfe in 1759. The French and Indian menace in New York was finally ended, and the colony entered a new phase of its development, with a newborn sense of its independent destiny.

With the outbreak of the Revolutionary War, New York once again became a vitally important strategic center of international military operations. No other colony knew so well the cost of freedom. Almost a third of the battles of the Revolution were fought on New York soil (including many of the most decisive), as blackened ruins along its valleys and frontiers made tragically clear before the peace was won. England's aim was to split the united colonies by winning control of the Hudson Valley with its important military routes to the north and west. It was the only large-scale offensive planned by the British Army during the war. Albany was the key point of control, but Albany was never taken. Any such possibility ended with Burgoyne's surrender to American troops at Saratoga in October 1777, the turning point of the Revolution and one of the truly decisive battles in history. With that impressive American victory England's master plan was frustrated. Encouraged by such a show of American strength and determination, France sent the troops and ships (and money) which so substantially contributed to the final triumph at Yorktown in 1781.

New Yorkers were seriously divided among themselves throughout the war. The state probably had the largest number of English Loyalists in the colonies, and the ground was bloodied by the civil strife of friends and neighbors, as at the decisive conflict at Oriskany—the most sanguinary battle of the Revolution.

Following Washington's retreat from Manhattan Island in 1776 the city of New York remained in British hands for seven years. It became a haven for Loyalists, who fled there from areas controlled by patriots. When, after formal negotiations, Washington reentered the city on November 25, 1783, the British officials and troops sailed off, taking with them thousands of hapless Loyalists and leaving a population only one-half as large as it had been before the war. During the occupation two major fires had destroyed many hundreds of the city's buildings. But the port of New York and the new state it served were destined for greatness, as developments in the coming decades would make abundantly clear.

In the year of the peace George Washington looked out over the liberated countryside and, with an eye for its beauty and its promise, he declared that it might become "the seat of empire." He bought a piece of its wilderness land in speculation. So did Alexander Hamilton, Robert Morris, and virtually everyone else with capital to risk or a new home to build. Stolid Dutch bankers, titled Englishmen, and distinguished French émigrés vied with Yankees, Yorkers, and naturalized countrymen in what was America's first real land rush. Fortunes were lost as well as made as a result of the frantic opportunism that spread across the state. The illustrious Robert Morris, "financier of the American Revolution," lost 150,000 acres through some bad decisions. He spent three years in debtor's prison and never recovered his fortune.

Long before the present boundaries of the state were settled, restless New Englanders had looked westward toward the promising country which in alien hands had threatened to contain them within their tight little corner of the New World. The colonists who had earlier spread along the Hudson Valley and ventured into the Mohawk Valley into Iroquois country, eyed the intruders from the East with reasonable suspicion (those "locusts of the West," as James Fenimore Cooper disdainfully called them). From the beginnings of settlement they watched these "Johnnies" from New England (Johnny-come-latelys, we would probably call them) edging their way across disputed borders. And since the Dutch word for Johnny is *Janke,* the intrusive newcomers became known as *Yankees.*

Before the end of the eighteenth century the westering stream of Yankees had swollen into a torrent. In sloops and sleighs, by oxcart and shanks' mare, they thronged the valley routes into the newly opened West. They were, as Thomas Carlyle once wrote Emerson, "tough as gutta-percha with *occult* unsubduable fire in their belly," and they were not to be denied. Early in the nineteenth century Timothy Dwight, austere president of Yale College, observed that New York was already in a fair way to become a Yankee "colony." He looked with solemn and pious satisfaction on the rich benefits that would thus accrue to the raw newborn state. "I know of no physical reason," he pronounced, "why the people of New York may not be as prosperous and happy as any on the globe."

We have not yet established a reliable measure for gauging human happiness. But in the next century and a half New York did become the most populous and prosperous state of the Union. A sharp spur to the Yankee invasion of New York came, it has been said, from the tall stalks of corn and grain and the jumbo-sized onions and potatoes sent "back home" by pioneering families from New England. A land that could yield such prodigies was a land that in good Puritan conscience must not be neglected. Within a generation what had been a virtually uninhabited wilderness was being worked into fruitful farmland that would soon produce more than it could consume, and into growing cities that processed and distributed the mounting harvests to other parts of the nation and the world.

The War of 1812 only briefly and marginally interfered with the state's western progress. It was a regrettable altercation for which New Yorkers showed only moderate enthusiasm. As late as 1814 several companies of militia quit their post at New York City in a body to go home to harvest their crops, as other troops had turned away from an invasion of Canada to defend their homes. Once again Britain threatened the borderlands, once again British forces stabbed down from the north toward Albany—and were turned back. In a surprising victory Commodore Thomas Macdonough repulsed the enemy forces at Plattsburgh Bay; Oliver Hazard Perry, with a fleet hastily built of green wood, at Put-in Bay won control of Lake Erie and the portal to the West.

It was in the end a futile and unnecessary war, but with its termination America felt its independence was lastingly secured, and New York could confidently resume its phenomenal growth. Freed from Britain's tight wartime blockade, the maritime traffic in and out of the port of New York swarmed to all parts of the globe. As its population quadrupled in the first twenty years of the nineteenth century, the city became indisputably "the great commercial emporium of America."

The state's economy could expand only as its transportation facilities improved and multiplied. Early in the century scores of companies were chartered to build toll turnpikes, and by 1821 four thousand miles of such roads had been completed, many of them fanning out from Albany, major crossroads of the state's commerce and general traffic. Stagecoach lines followed the Albany Post Road along the Hudson Valley to and from New York City. When in 1807 Robert Fulton's *North River Steamboat of Clermont,* popularly known as the *Clermont,* thrashed its

way up the Hudson at the rate of five miles an hour, "like the devil in a sawmill," a brand new era of transportation was opened. It was a turning point of history. By 1846 there were at least one hundred steamboats plying the river, bulging with passengers and freight, and others had ventured out into the open water along the Atlantic coast.

To tap the immeasurable resources of the western country, cheaper and more commodious transport than wagons and coaches could provide was essential. The War of 1812 had postponed construction of the proposed Erie Canal that would connect Albany with Buffalo and the Great Lakes; the war also emphasized the need for such a navigable water route to run east and west through the heart of the state. The stupendous and revolutionary project was undertaken in 1817 and completed in 1825, to the astonishment of many skeptics (Thomas Jefferson among them). "America can never forget," boasted one prominent New York citizen, "that we have built the longest canal in the least time, with the least experience, for the least money, and to the greatest public benefit."

The benefits were manifold. Freight rates between Buffalo and Albany almost immediately dropped by 90 percent. Shipping time between those two cities was reduced from twenty days to eight. With eastern markets now so much easier and cheaper to reach, western farmers could sensibly develop cash crops for distant city-dwellers. (In 1827 the governor of Georgia complained that wheat from central New York was being sold at Savannah more cheaply than wheat from central Georgia.) New York quickly became the foremost agricultural state in the United States. The phenomenal success of the Erie encouraged the construction of lateral canals running both north and south to feed that main artery—and new areas of the state were opened to economic development.

In New York, as elsewhere in the country, the British blockade of American ports during the War of 1812 had fostered the development of domestic manufactures. With the ready access to raw materials provided by the canal, with ample water power, with a rapidly increasing population demanding ever more consumer goods, and with both capital and labor in ample supply, the state also soon led the nation in industrial output. In the course of a brief generation it had grown to justify beyond dispute Washington's term, the "seat of empire."

No sooner was the canal completed than railroads started threading their way across the countryside—first as abbreviated feeders to the canal from outlying districts, then gradually as separate carriers in their own right, linking communities and areas beyond effective reach of the canal. The Mohawk and Hudson, running a twenty-eight-mile stretch between the canal terminus at Schenectady and the river port of Albany, was chartered in 1826—the first railroad to be chartered in the United States, although not the first to operate. Consolidating the bits and pieces of track into a binding network of rails, dominated by the lines of the Erie and the New York Central, required decades of financial and political manipulation in which such celebrated—and notorious—individuals as "Commodore" Cornelius Vanderbilt, Daniel Drew, Jay Gould, and Jim Fisk played their important roles. In 1851 cars of the Erie carried the Cabinet of President Millard Fillmore across the state to western New York, over the longest continuous railroad line in the world. (The day that line opened, Daniel Webster had crossed the state in a rocking chair fastened to a flatcar, with wildly cheering crowds to speed his way.) Those iron rails cemented New York's grip on trade with the West. Before the Civil War put new strains on its ways and means, the state had the finest transportation system in the country.

In spite of ever-mounting competition from the railroads, the canals as late as 1872 still carried a peak load of 6 million tons of freight. And in the meantime, the natural waterways of the state—its lakes, rivers, sound, and coastal waters—carried a volume of cargo far exceeding that of the canals and railroads combined.

In the meantime also, the explosive growth of the state in almost every direction called for adjustments in its political, financial, and social structure to accommodate rapidly and constantly changing circumstances. As small farmers settled the land, so many of them transplanted New Englanders with Yankee notions, they challenged the long-established position of the large landholders. In 1835 James Fenimore Cooper complained that these unwanted interlopers were "lacerating" the woodlands about the ample estate his father had so comfortably established at Cooperstown, on the shores of Lake Otsego.

Along with the Yankees came immigrant hordes from overseas who took over the abandoned farms of those who had pushed farther west and helped to swell the population of cities throughout much of the state. The prospects of both groups were furthered when, in 1821, a state constitutional convention (led largely by men who had come from New England) gave the unqualified right to vote to all white males over twenty-one years of age. Six years later slavery was abolished in the state. Another constitutional convention, in 1846, brought further democratic reforms. By then the traditional manorial system had been all but destroyed by the popular will. Such an anachronistic survival of feudal aristocracy had no plausible place in the years during and following Andrew Jackson's Presidency.

State politics in the second quarter of the nineteenth century was largely controlled by the so-called Albany Regency, an informal group of leaders of the Democratic party who partly controlled elections through the spoils system and strictly enforced party regularity. One of those principal figures was Martin Van Buren. Van Buren had played a prominent role in the constitutional convention of 1821, became governor of the state in 1828, and then succeeded Andrew Jackson as President of the United States in 1836. His consummate political skill earned him the sobriquet "Little Magician," and his influence helped to give shape to what became the modern Democratic party.

Van Buren's principal opponent in the state was Thurlow Weed, another astute politician, whose distrust of Jacksonian democracy led him to form a coalition group of more conservative bent, which identified itself with the national organization known as the Whig party. In 1840 the Whigs' candidate for president, William Henry Harrison, was elected; its candidate for governor of New York, Weed's close associate William H. Seward, had won that office in 1838. With the disruption of the Whig party, both Weed and Seward swung over to the new Republican party, formed in 1854. Seward long remained New York's most vocal critic of slavery, an institution which in 1858 he referred to as leading toward "an irrepressible conflict between opposing and enduring forces," a phrase that caught the public imagination. He lived on to assume a dominant role in Lincoln's wartime

Cabinet—and subsequently to negotiate the purchase of Alaska from Russia, a historically memorable deal, commonly referred to at the time as "Seward's Folly."

The fortunes of the Whig party while it flourished were substantially benefited by a powerful press that supported its policies, notably by the New York *Tribune,* which was founded by Horace Greeley in 1840 and soon enjoyed a national reputation. Under Greeley's direction the *Tribune*'s editorial page became one of the most popular and influential forces in the history of American journalism. The prestige of the paper and its editor attracted such notable talents as Margaret Fuller, author, critic, and social reformer, the first woman to work as a foreign correspondent for the press; George Ripley, who as literary critic recognized and remarked upon the most significant books published in the United States; and the celebrated world traveler Bayard Taylor. The *Tribune*'s managing editor from 1847 to 1862, Charles Anderson Dana, became almost as influential as Greeley. Upstate New York proliferated with newspapers of its own, including such distinguished examples as the Albany *Argus* and *Evening Journal,* each of which spoke with authority and interest for important segments of the state's population and had an impact on the political and social development of New York.

But New York City became and remained the hub of American journalism, as of so many other enterprises. In 1825 William Cullen Bryant came to the city from Great Barrington, Massachusetts, to escape the factiousness of small-town New England life and to pursue the literary career he had already started (as Captain R. H. Macy came there from Nantucket to advance his commercial career with a pioneering little store in Manhattan—and James Spencer Morgan from Hartford, Connecticut, to explore the possibilities of the banking business). For more than fifty years Bryant preached liberalism from the editorial pages of the *Evening Post,* which became one of the leading Democratic journals of the country. In 1851 the enduring New York *Times* was founded as a counter to Greeley's *Tribune* and soon surpassed that paper with its circulation, priding itself then as it has ever since for its news coverage of foreign affairs. Technological advances (and shrewd merchandising) had long since introduced the penny press, which brought the daily news, along with scandal and other forms of sensational trivia, within reach of even the most indigent of the population. The first of such cheap and popular journals, the New York *Sun,* was founded in 1833 by Benjamin Day, who some years later published Edgar Allan Poe's fictitious account of the aerial crossing of the Atlantic as a "straight" story—one which brought crowds of gullible and excited people swarming to the paper's offices for further details. Day also published Poe's poem "The Raven," which in an entirely different fashion also created an overnight sensation. At every level the New York press was an important factor in shaping popular opinion and taste, not only in the state but in other regions of the nation.

Triggered in part by stories and editorials in the press, in part by the driving edge of New England morality, and in part by a ferment of ideas rising from a lively intercourse among people of different backgrounds and traditions, a spirit of reform and experiment swept through the state during the decades immediately preceding the Civil War. That was not a local phenomenon; for reformers and humanitarians of every stripe America at large offered a richly endowed laboratory for correcting the old evils of society and for rehearsing new solutions to the eternal problems of human existence. (As Emerson wrote Carlyle in 1840, "we are all a little wild here with numberless projects of social reform.")

However, New York provided a particularly lively stage for such demonstrations, which were undertaken both in the name of reason and in the face of it. In a land so steeped in heroic legends, a land which had witnessed the all-but-legendary achievement of the Erie Canal, and which in so many other ways had assumed leadership among the states of the Union, almost anything came to seem possible—even the final redemption of man. Temperance, the abolition of slavery, and women's rights were only a few of the uplifting causes that attracted vigorous advocates and adherents within the state. It was on a New York hillside that Joseph Smith found the Book of Mormon that opened into a new world of religion for his followers—whom he led to a final sanctuary in Utah as their unusual faith met opposition in the East. In 1844 William Miller led his own faithful followers to another New York hillside to await the crack of doom which, he persuaded them by his intricate calculations, would happen on a certain night of that year. Garbed in their ascension robes, the expectant congregation waited in vain. At New Lebanon and John's Bay, the Shakers, followers of the eighteenth-century English immigrant Ann Lee, established communities whose members practiced celibacy and nonresistance, believed in full equality for women, and sought perfection in the pursuits of daily life—a perfectionism duly appreciated by today's collectors of Shaker crafts.

It was during those same prewar decades that New York experienced a remarkable upsurge of artistic activity. Americans were clamoring for a native art that would suggest the unlimited abundance and wonder of the American scene, and they got what they wanted from what came to be called the Hudson River school of painters. The work of the group, which included such skilled artists as Thomas Cole, Asher B. Durand, John F. Kensett, and Frederick E. Church, marked the beginnings of a significant American tradition in landscape painting. Their faithful rendering of the hills and lakes, the valleys and rivers of New York called attention to the still semiwild grandeur of the land, as Washington Irving, James Fenimore Cooper, and William Cullen Bryant were celebrating it in their stories and poems. Their influence lasted well into the postwar years and reached far beyond the confines of the state.

While those landscapists and seascapists were so actively and so agreeably charting the mountains and woodlands, the waterways and coasts of the state, other artists, such as the Long Islander William Sidney Mount, were making a vivid pictorial record of their provincial friends and neighbors at work, at rest, and at play, painted with understanding and with humor. Mount's formula for success in his art was simple enough: "Paint pictures that will take with the public—never paint for the few, but the many." That formula was extended in another dimension when Mount's more popular paintings were reproduced in inexpensive lithographic copies. In 1835 the New York firm of Nathaniel Currier, later to become Currier and Ives, issued its first lithograph—the first in a series of more than 4,300 subjects which over the next several generations, at prices from twenty cents to $3.00

each, won a wide distribution throughout the Atlantic world, far beyond the precincts of New York.

As it did in most of the states of the beleaguered Union, the Civil War brought profound changes to New York. The state provided no battlefields in this war as it had in earlier ones. But as the most wealthy and populous state, it paid the largest sums in taxes and war relief, sent the greatest number of men into the Union army—almost a half million—and lost more men in battle than any other state. (One third of the men who fell in the defeat of Bull Run on July 2, 1861, came from New York City.) More than forty New Yorkers became generals in the Union Army. By their willingness to serve in the armed forces, and their courage on the battlefields, immigrants of Irish and German origin who served in the ranks won a new tolerance from their fellow countrymen.

The closing of the Mississippi River to traffic from the North greatly increased the tonnage of freight and produce carried by New York's railroads and floated by the Erie Canal. The latter, indeed, became the greatest inland water passage in the world. War also imposed greater demands on the New York farmer to provide the supplies of wheat, wool, and dairy and meat products required by the North's gigantic military machine, as well as by the civilian population on the home front. The rural population of the state was decreasing, but the progressive mechanization of agriculture was rapidly increasing the seasonal output of the individual farmer. At that, farmers constituted the largest occupational group in the state, and for a while yet the number and value of farms in New York exceeded the figures for any other state. The major wheat-producing lands now lay in the Midwest, but their yield was to a large degree funneled through New York to domestic and foreign markets. In the course of that transport Buffalo became a major port, linking West with East, as it had already become the greatest inland port in the world for immigrants in passage. Even while the war was in progress, vessels left New York Harbor with their holds crammed with wheat destined for English and European ports. The spectacle of a nation fighting a great war with large numbers of its young farmers in military service, and producing such a surplus of foodstuffs at the same time, seemed to contradict all logic, as the English novelist

Anthony Trollope, visiting America at the time, remarked with astonishment.

In spite of its patriotic services and its other practical accomplishments, New York was by no means united in its support of the northern cause, or in the way the northern cause was being directed. Some citizens, principally from the Democratic party, opposed the war so vehemently that they were accused of disloyalty, or at least of hampering the war effort. Republicans, in turn, were accused by their opponents of violating civil rights. The most serious disagreements arose over the administration of the conscription act passed by Congress in March 1863. In July of that year, as the draft was about to begin in New York City, protesting mobs rioted through the streets, sacking and looting and burning property as they went. For good measure stray blacks were lynched. New York has never experienced such violent disruption of law and order, of justice and mercy, as it suffered during those three chaotic days.

New York emerged from the war enriched, and more aggressive than ever in its role as the Empire State. During the conflict, its industries had been sharply stimulated; its businesses had become bigger businesses, its financial operations had brought an unprecedented concentration of wealth into the hands of its bankers and corporation directors. A pattern of economic growth had been established that would give shape to developments for a century and more to come. Unfortunately, the glittering possibilities of gain that goaded the state to almost frenetic activity opened the door to venality in politics and business alike, and made shameful history for decades. The humanitarianism and idealism of prewar years, odd as their manifestations sometimes were, gave way to cynicism and opportunism that brought fat profits to those of unscrupulous greed, misery to the many they exploited, and gross discredit to the spirit of American democracy. Once again the circumstances were not unique to New York, but they emphatically underlined the breakdown of moral standards that afflicted the nation during the administration of President Ulysses S. Grant.

Under the dominating influence of William Marcy ("Boss") Tweed, leader of Tammany Hall, political corruption infested virtually every aspect of state and local government. Before Tweed and members of his ring landed in jail, they had swindled New York City alone out of scores of millions of dollars in one way and another. Big business controlled politics, and the party boss in effect controlled the questionable franchises and other highly remunerative concessions that promised him the most graft in return. Voters could be bought or ballot boxes stuffed to elect the boss's choice for public office, and so on in a sordid succession of looting operations that fed the ring's omnivorous treasury. Upstate Republicans were as corrupt as Tammany Democrats. New York politics was to a disgraceful degree a business whose profits could be as large as they were illicit.

Tweed's power was broken largely through the efforts of Samuel J. Tilden, another Democratic leader but one of a different stripe (with substantial help from the series of devastating cartoons drawn by Thomas Nast for *Harper's Weekly*). Tilden's reputation as a reformer in the name of good government won him the governor's office in 1874 and then, two years later, almost won him the presidency. Unfortunately, his election did not end the evils of machine-run politics in the state. It did, however, herald the subsequent enlightened administrations of such governors as Grover Cleveland, Theodore Roosevelt, Charles Evans Hughes, and Alfred E. Smith, which progressively raised the quality of politics in New York to the relatively high level that has been generally sustained for the past fifty years. Under the leadership of its succession of capable governors, as has fairly been claimed, New York has set the pace for all other states, and served as "the incubator of inventive ideas later adopted for the nation as a whole." As a matter of record, six New Yorkers advanced from governmental posts in the state to the Presidency of the United States, and nine have served as the nation's Vice Presidents.

The problems with which New York's government had to contend in the years following the Civil War did not change so much as they intensified. Decade by decade, immigrant hordes continued to use the port of New York as the principal gateway to the New World, many of them moving on through the industrial belt extending up the Hudson Valley and westward to Lake Erie, and many of those settling along the route to help make that twenty-five-mile-wide corridor by far the most populous area of the state. For almost 150 years—from about 1820 until the 1960s—New York remained both the most populous and the most cosmopolitan state in the Union. If, as has been said, New Yorkers are much like other people, it is because so many of them have been and are "other" people —from New England and other neighboring states, from Ireland, Germany, Italy, Poland, Russia, among many other lands, and more lately in large numbers from the American South and Puerto Rico.

That ethnic diversity is manifest in the large number of foreign-language newspapers and periodicals—including those in Chinese, Arabic, Albanian, Greek, Hungarian, French, German, and Italian—that are published in the state. It can also be seen on the face of the land. Thus, the eastern limits of the state, where the twin flukes of Long Island reach out into the Atlantic Ocean, still retain some of the character of an early New England settlement—with saltwater habits; trim, long-weathered buildings; and lingering patterns of Yankee speech—while 300 miles to the west as the crow flies (more than 450 miles by commonly traveled surface routes), where the winds roar in off the Great Lakes, immigrant millworkers from central Europe learn English with a midwestern accent in the inland port of Buffalo.

Many of the cities that early sprang to life along that corridor with the opening of the Erie Canal, mushroomed into spreading metropolitan areas which in time developed that oscillating rhythm of industrial concentration and suburban expansion so common to a large part of the American scene today. More than a million people, including one of the largest Polish populations in the world, have congregated within thirty miles of Buffalo's steel foundries, grain elevators, and other plants. Across the state to the east, the General Electric Company's major headquarters in Schenectady is virtually a city in itself, with its miles of streets, its scores of buildings, and its many thousand employees. At the midpoint of the last century, Rochester (originally the home of the Seneca Indians), close to the mouth of the Genesee River at Lake Ontario, proudly compared its massive flour mills with the most enduring monuments of ancient Egypt. As the principal wheatfields of the nation moved farther west, the city turned its industrial activity in other directions. The internationally renowned optical firm, Bausch and Lomb Company, was organized there in 1880, as George Eastman, a local bank clerk, was developing another firm which in 1888 introduced the Kodak camera, with spectacular consequences. In years to come, "Kodak City's" particular bent for cosmopolitan culture has been by no means discouraged by the many Italians and Germans who settled there.

It is invidious to single out these particular centers of growth and production, but a complete record of the state's industrial growth would exhaust more pages than remain in this book. The point of basic importance is that in the course of the last century New Yorkers have become engaged in virtually every kind of manufacture listed by the United States Census Bureau, a range of industrial activity that gives the state a large measure of its economic stability. More people are engaged in more varied manufacturing than in any other state, and more money is involved in the payrolls of manufacturing firms.

Although New York became the leading industrial and commercial state of the nation and became increasingly urbanized, its farmland continued—and continues to this day—to produce abundant harvests around the seasons. Dairy farming was firmly established in New York at an early date. In the years following Appomattox the state developed into one of the most productive dairy lands in America. Today milk flows by tank car and truck from wide areas of the state to the large consuming market of its cities.

No one who has traveled through the state during the March and April thaws will forget the pleasant and ubiquitous sight of sugar maple trees draining their sap into waiting buckets. Almost two hundred years ago more than a few speculators dreamed of supplying the wide world with the sweets that could be derived from the produce of such groves. Those high expectations were hardly realized, but New York has never ceased harvesting ample "crops" from its maple trees. (As a symbol of that traditional practice, the sugar maple has been chosen the state tree.) In later years the bulk of their large yields goes just beyond the state border to be sold as "good old" Vermont maple syrup and sugar.

In May the great clouds of blossoms along the Hudson and Champlain valleys and in the Great Lakes plain foretell an abundant harvest of apples. Until there were adequate transportation facilities such fruit went to the hogs for food, or to the cider press for as little as a half dollar a barrel. By 1870, however, Oneida County was shipping nearly eighteen-thousand barrels of apples to city markets by canal or railroad— varieties of the fruit that had been vastly improved through the efforts of the state's horticultural societies. The average annual yield in recent years has been second only to that of the state of Washington.

The immigrants from other countries who moved across the state in the wake of Dutch and Yankee pioneers were prepared to work the land (as well as to man the factories) with the same firm purpose as their predecessors— and to retrieve it where it had been improvidently used. In the summer, close-gardening farmers of Polish and Italian descent take from the rich mucklands of the central state—land in this case reclaimed from swamps by these persistent cultivators—the nation's largest onion crop, along with other produce. Also during the summer months, not far from Long Island's abundant potato fields, ducks in the millions crowd the shores and coves of Suffolk County nurtured for their ultimate place on dinner menus throughout the country. And around the calendar, in cool cellars dug deep into the hills that cradle Pleasant Valley, Concord, Catawba, Niagara, and Delaware grapes from neighboring vineyards are transmuted into wines that bear proud labels. Here again, in the years following the Civil War, immigrants from European wine-growing districts brought special skills. By the turn of the century New York wines were listed by restaurants and hotels across the country, as they still are.

As in the case of industry, the diversity of agriculture in New York has contributed to the state's relatively stable economic structure. As Timothy Dwight long ago said they might, the people of the state have come to happy terms with the land they live on. They have at times abused its welcome, as did the lumbering gangs that in the last century threatened to skin the Adirondacks and other forested regions of their covering of virgin timber, and that did in fact make New York for a while the foremost lumbering state in the Union. There are still lumbermen in the Adirondacks, and the mountains are ringed about with mills that produce prodigious quantities of paper and paperboard. But to-

day much of the pulp that supplies those mills comes from across the Canadian border or from overseas.

In 1885 the state legislature passed a law establishing forest preserves in the Adirondack and Catskill Mountains. Nine years later, a further safeguard was written into the state constitution, providing that those preserves "shall be forever kept as wild forest lands." The old scars left by past misuse are healing and the protected areas, with their glinting lakes and sparkling streams, have become the largest such reservation in the nation. The Adirondack State Park alone is more extensive than the combined areas of Yellowstone, Yosemite, Grand Canyon, and Olympia National Parks. Since timber cutting was stopped, other large areas flanking the Hudson River have been growing ever more wild. In portions of the Hudson Highlands this wilderness is within view of the towering piles of New York City—the most extensive wild area in the world so close to a major metropolis.

Better to serve its farms and factories, as well as the general welfare of its inhabitants, New York has multiplied and modernized its transportation facilities as needs grew. With competition from the railroads, the old Erie Canal became inadequate, fell into disuse, and was finally closed. In its place the state built a new barge canal which started operations in 1918 and in recent years has been carrying about 5 million tons of freight annually. By 1900 the railroads (which had been spread across the state at the expense of such scandalous buccaneering as the nation has rarely witnessed) reached the peak of their supremacy and they in turn have been progressively challenged by automotive transport. In the 1950s the state built its colossal Thruway, described as "the world's greatest highway," which closely parallels the route of the Hudson River and Erie Canal; there are no sharp curves, crossroads, traffic lights, or steep inclines along its 427-mile length. Its construction was a gigantic engineering accomplishment, rivaling in its own time the magnitude and consequence of the efforts that had created the Erie more than a century earlier. (As an interesting sidelight to the influence of an improved highway system, in 1975 California was receiving more than half its imports through the port of New York, imports which were then carried west by truck.)

In the Southern Tier of New York, such large industries as the International Business Machines Corporation at Endicott send heavy air freight to all parts of the country, bypassing the problems of topography altogether. Along the northern margin of the state, the most drastic surgery ever performed on the North American continent formed the St. Lawrence Seaway, a cooperative venture with Canada. The Seaway has been designed to bring that part of New York, and the entire Midwest, closer by direct sea route to major European ports than either New York or Philadelphia is, as well as to supply large new sources of power.

In the decade following the War of 1812 the volume of its maritime traffic increased to the point where the port of New York, with its adjacent facilities in New Jersey, became indisputably the most active in the United States. It has never yielded its preeminence. The metropolis is a seaborne city, the center of a web of far-reaching waterways and the commanding post of an ocean harbor that provides the most enticing natural entrance to the North Atlantic continent. According to the 1970 federal census, the total yearly value of imports and exports cleared by the Port Authority of New York and New Jersey was $20 billion, twice that of any other American port—and that value has reportedly been sizably increased in the meantime. The history of such a seaport cannot be told in local terms, for from an early date its affairs have reached out directly to all points of the globe. In 1975 approximately a third of its imports came from Europe; almost 16 percent from the Far East; about 5 percent from Africa; almost 10 percent each from South America and Australasia; 12 percent from the Mediterranean; and about 15 percent from North America. Exports through the port follow a roughly similar pattern of worldwide interest, although with some significant variations; the largest volume goes to the most remote parts of the earth in the Far East, and a much-reduced percentage to other parts of North America.

It is possible to live in the narrow confines of Manhattan Island, the hub of New York and the smallest of its five boroughs, hemmed in by mortar and brick, and remain unaware of the lick of the waters at the ends of its short crosstown streets. New York's long and continuing status as a great metropolis has overshadowed its equal rise as the world's greatest seaport. Almost half the people who live in the Empire State are crowded into the relatively minute fraction of its total area at its extreme southern limit, metropolitan New York. The metropolitan concentrate is politically integrated with the rest of the state's population, but in a usually strained and distrustful relationship with "upstate" government, from which it habitually claims it receives a disproportionately small share of revenue in return for the amount of taxes it provides.

It contributes abundantly to most of the statistics that give the state such an impressive rating in atlases and almanacs. But by those who live beyond its confines, the metropolis is commonly regarded as a "foreign" entity, albeit one with which they have obviously managed to coexist on favorable terms.

Some years ago Dr. John Finley, a sage editor of the New York *Times,* referred to this strange alliance of city and state governments as the United States of New York, a phrase that aptly suggests the relationship of the two disparate elements, upstate and metropolis. Each has a population that in itself is larger than that of all but a few other states. With more regard for logical theory than for constitutional practice, it has frequently been suggested that the city be established as a separate state. However, New York City has also become the direct center of a megalopolis, extending from Boston to Washington. The New York metropolitan region alone contains parts of three states, almost three hundred other communities, and the rural regions that lie between—a supercommunity whose people read the same newspapers, frequent or are dependent upon the same principal trading and distribution center, and face common problems of public concern, although they maintain separate governments.

New York is the greatest city to develop in modern times, but unlike other great cities—Rome, Paris, London—it has left practically no physical trace of its origins or of the stages of its spectacular growth. No other city has so enthusiastically dedicated itself to constant change as a positive guiding principle. No city in history has shown such indifference to the monuments of its past. There is far less standing of colonial New York, for example, than there is of Periclean Athens. It might be said that the city's nostalgia is not for what has been but for what is yet to come. The skyline of New York—that chaotic, jagged, and preposterously beautiful outline of the city's towering buildings—is far more than evidence of engineering skills and "engineered" real estate values; it is a dominant symbol of our New World civilization, the shifting graph of modern man's busiest dreams. And New York has long since become so indisputably the most important and largest city in the United States that, as one observer has noted, it alone among all the striving young cities of America can afford to call itself both *little* and *old.*

As slightly confused visitors continue to insist, "little old New York" is not typical of America. It is not typical of anything, for there is nothing quite like it in the world. But with its all-American population and the extreme diversity of its activities and interests, the city does reflect the attitudes, the economy, and the culture of the nation at large. It is a nerve center energized by impulses and by people from all over the land, and it feeds back its synthesis of America, for better or for worse, through its vast publishing enterprises, its theaters, its television networks, its museums, and other nationally influential mediums of communication.

Even this brief summary may suggest that the state of New York is a house of many mansions. Throughout its history it has meant many different things to many different people. In important ways its development over the centuries clearly reflects the changing patterns of life in America at large. The sobriquet "Empire State" has been well earned.

*A Pictorial History*

The first white man known to have visited New York was the Florentine navigator Giovanni da Verrazzano. Sailing at the behest of Francis I, king of France, in search of a passage to Asia, in 1524 the Italian entered New York Bay through which, he reported, "flowed to the sea a very great river." Eighty-five years later, the Frenchman Samuel de Champlain (1) entered what is now New York State from his base at Quebec to the north. At Ticonderoga, by the lake that now bears his name, eager to forge friendships with native tribes, Champlain helped the Algonquins defeat the Iroquois (2), whose lasting enmity the French thereby earned. Had Champlain chosen to follow the Indian trails south along the Hudson, Henry Hudson might have found the lilies of France waving a greeting from Manhattan Island when he arrived there later that same season in his little ship, the *Half-Moon,* shown here in a model (3). As it happened, Hudson was the harbinger of the stream of Dutch settlers soon to follow. In the autumn of 1614, in the interest of merchants appealing for exclusive trading rights in this newly explored country, Holland's States General was presented with a map on which for the first time Manhattan Island and the name *New Netherland* appeared (4). It had been prepared from a survey made the preceding season by one Adrian Block.

The Indians who greeted the first explorers along the lower Hudson River valley were Algonquins. Some unidentified artist painted what has been described as a family group of such tribesmen from the region of Manhattan Island (1). Other, more or less fanciful pictures of these natives paddling out to greet the white man in their fur-laden canoes appear in the earliest engraved views of New Amsterdam (2). The Iroquois played the greatest role in the Indian history of what is now New York State. They had settled in central New York as five separate nations which, according to Indian tradition, had been brought together in the late sixteenth century by Hiawatha and Dekanawida as a union or confederacy, known to them as the "long house." Their principal habitations were, in fact, long houses, bark-covered huts about twenty feet wide and one hundred or more feet long, models of which have been reconstructed (3). For protection, stockades of upright logs twenty or thirty feet tall were built, as can be seen in depictions on early engraved maps of the area (4). Villages were moved about every ten years or so to places where more favorable hunting might be found, and fresh soil to till for corn, tobacco, squash, and beans. A crude illustration dating from about 1700 shows an Iroquois warrior, his skin painted in boldly designed patterns, burning an enemy lodge (5), bottom. The lands occupied by the so-called Five Nations were depicted in a map drawn in 1700 (6).

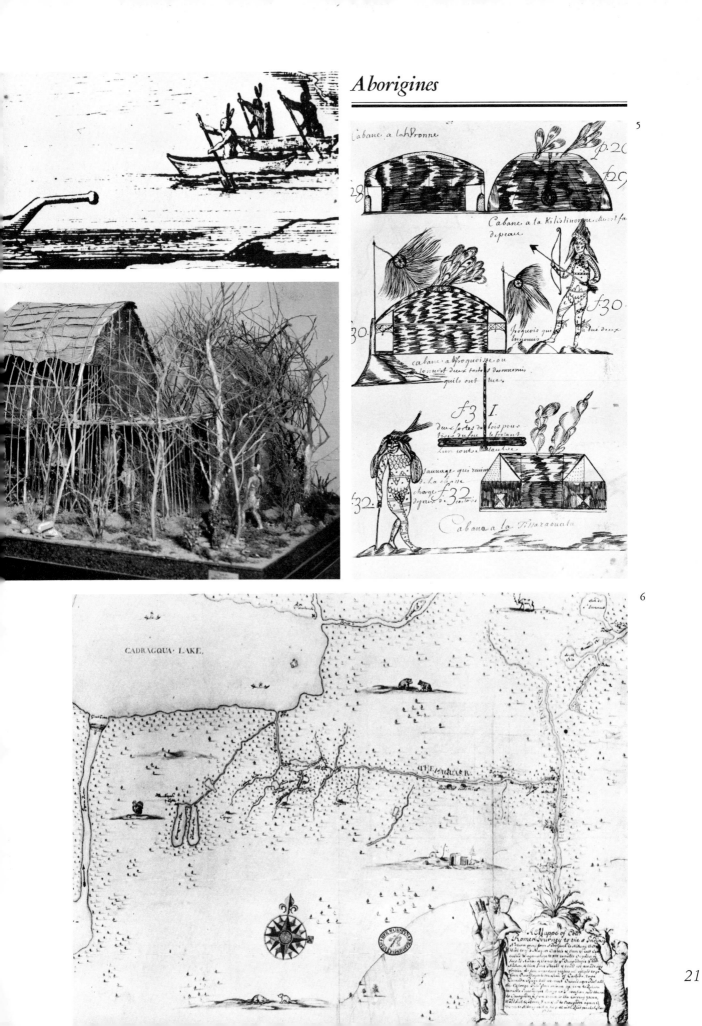

*t' Fort nieúw Amsterdam op de*

## Dutch New York

In 1626 it was reported to the States General that Peter Minuit, director general of New Netherland, had bought Manhattan Island from "the wild men [the native Indians], for the value of sixty guilders." About that time the earliest known view of New Amsterdam was drawn (1), probably intended primarily to show the directors of the West India Company the proposed location of a fort with five bastions (as built, the fort had four). The view depicts about thirty houses in the little colony, a windmill, and a stone-walled counting-house. A copy of an annotated map made in 1639 (2) represents the first actual survey of Manhattan Island with all its important topographical features, its rudimentary road system, and the farms of the early settlers, as well as adjoining farms on Staten Island and Long Island, in the Bronx, and in New Jersey. A detail from another map issued about 1648 (3) shows the course of the Hudson River along which Dutch settlements had clustered as the seventeenth century advanced. Only a few years later, in 1651, a map was issued in London which traced the Hudson River bending westward and, after filtering through "a mighty great lake," finding its way by this northwest passage to "the sea of China and the Indies" (4). At the end of the seventeenth century appeared the earliest known view of Niagara Falls (5), which had been discovered by the friar Louis Hennepin while preparing for an epic voyage down the Mississippi.

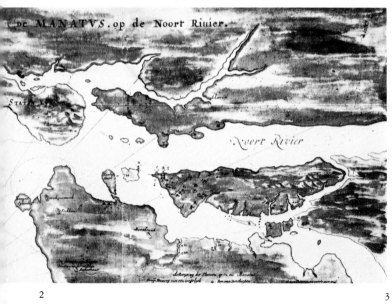

DE MANATVS. op de Noort Riuier.

*Noort Rivier*

2

3

Nouа
Francia

4

new.

MARY LAND
Lord Baltimore Plantation
begun 1635.

Swee ds Holl a d
Plant at: Plant
Ascion
Noua Albion

200 miles

Uh river

Elk river

Tankard River

this River the Lord Ba: ... hath a Patent in it and hath a great of Furrs

but the Swedes are planted in it

Ridiuck woods

Hantcok

This River the Dutch have a plantation and

A great trade of Furrs

Roritas

5

## Dutch Cities in the Wilderness

One of the earliest views of New Amsterdam's skyline, dating from about 1650 (1), shows the "pretty large stone church" within the fort, its belfry rising above the surrounding rooftops. About that time a visitor observed that the settlement on Manhattan Island was but "the commencement of a town to be built there." As the seventeenth century progressed the town did indeed develop into a small but true replica of a typical Dutch town (2), with its canal running through the heart of the community, its neat gardens and orchards, its houses of brick and tile with stepped gables. Thus it may be recognized in a meticulous redraft of an aerial plan of the city made in 1660 (3). The illustration depicts about three hundred dwellings, among other structures, hemmed in on the tip of Manhattan by a protective wall (the future Wall Street), with Broadway running from the fort out into the countryside beyond the wall. Near the water's edge the City Tavern, which opened to the public in 1642, soon became New Amsterdam's first City Hall (4). Upriver Albany was much the same. Even as late as the mid-eighteenth century, according to one report, there were about four thousand inhabitants, "mostly Dutch or of Dutch extract. . . . Their whole thoughts being turned upon profit and gain which necessarily makes them live retired and frugall." As a reminder of that earlier scene, the seventeenth-century Dutch governor's house was still standing in the early nineteenth century (5).

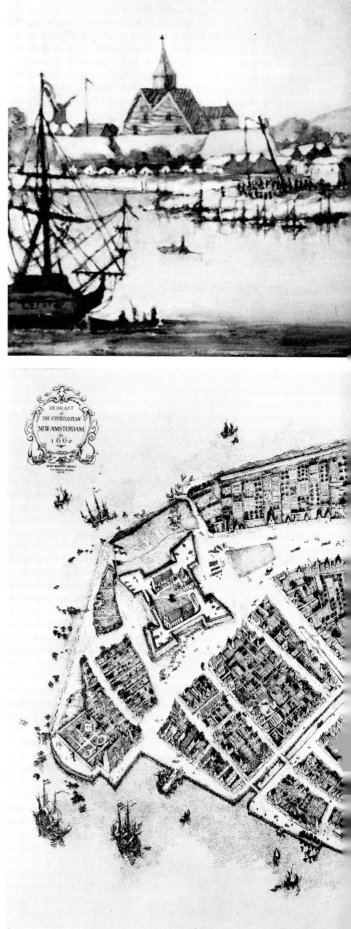

2

4

5

1    2

3

4

5

6

Indoors as well as out of doors the colonists of New Netherland reproduced as best they could the atmosphere of their homeland. Beds were arranged in alcoves behind curtains, as in the reconstructed house of the ferry keeper at the Van Cortlandt Manor (1). "You may go thro all the rooms of a great house," one traveler reported in Albany, "and never see a bed. . . ." Also in typical Dutch style, doors were divided in two horizontally, like this one at Philipsburg Manor (2). The great cupboard, or *kas,* indispensable storage facility of a Dutch home, was reproduced, often with painted imitation of the richly carved decoration of European models (3)—probably the first still-life paintings done in America. The engraving on a silver beaker (4) made by Cornelius Vandenburgh, the first native-born smith, copied illustrations from the fables of the Dutch author Jacobus Cats, which were popular on both sides of the Atlantic (5). The earliest known colonial teakettle (tea was a relatively novel and expensive drink at the time) was fashioned by the New York silversmith Cornelius Kierstede in the first decade of the eighteenth century (6).

Unlike their typical New England contemporaries, the Dutch settlers in the Hudson River valley were not averse to religious subjects in the painted decorations of their houses and churches. A bench fashioned in 1702 (1) bears a scene of the Last Judgment, with an appropriate verse in Dutch script admonishing that "there is still time to leave folly" before God's final judgment. In 1782, when he visited a house in Newburgh, New York, "built in the Dutch fashion," the Marquis de Chastellux noted that "the fire is in the room itself." A restored setting in the Museum of the City of New York gives a fair impression of such an early interior (2). Glazed earthenware Delft tiles (3), decorated with profane as well as religious subjects, were commonly used as facings for the large, jambless, hooded fireplaces; mantel ruffles kept smoke from spilling into the room. The stout-bottomed Dutch burghers so affectionately caricatured by Washington Irving would have found ample accommodations in one of the rare chairs surviving from early New York (4). The overmantel painted panel still survives to recall the farmhouse built in 1729 at Leeds, in the Catskills, for one Marten Van Bergen, obviously a person of Dutch origin or descent (5). As the artist recorded the scene, the barn, haystack (with an adjustable "roof"), cattle, sheep, chickens, laden wagon, and complement of people of both sexes and all ages, suggest the early farmer's varied life.

1

2

From the earliest days, men of many other lands mingled with the Dutch along the Hudson River. As early as 1644 one observer heard as many as eighteen different languages spoken in New Amsterdam alone. Among the few houses that survive from the seventeenth century there is some indication of that diversity. In 1663 Pieter Bronck, son of a Danish settler (who gave his name to The Bronx), built a stone house at Coxsackie, to which he made additions in 1685 (1). The Bronck family lived here until 1939. Late in the seventeenth century, the Huguenot Jean Hasbrouck built a stone-and-clapboard house with a steep-pitched roof at New Paltz (2); it is one of five early dwellings that line what is said to be the oldest street in America with its original houses. In 1660, far out on Long Island, at East Hampton, Robert Dayton built a wooden saltbox house of the sort familiar to the English settlers of Massachusetts and Connecticut (3). This was to be the birthplace of John Howard Payne and his boyhood "Home, Sweet Home." A limestone-and-brick house built in 1676 by Colonel Wessel Ten Broeck at Kingston (4), became the meeting place of the first publicly elected New York Senate in 1777. On Staten Island, the oldest section of the only remaining house built there during the New Netherlands period dates from 1662 (5). It was raised by a French Walloon settler Pierre Billiou.

3

## New World Dutchmen

In his genial, satirical stories Washington Irving created an enduring image of the typical New Netherlander as a slow-witted, fat, pipe-smoking tippler. No one familiar with the bustling citizens of New Amsterdam and Albany and their families would have recognized such a caricature. Peter Stuyvesant (1), director general of New Netherland from 1646 to 1664, had lost a leg in colonial warfare in the West Indies before coming to Manhattan where, with a wooden leg ornamented with silver bands, he ruled with martial severity. He also conquered New Sweden, before his colony was in turn taken over by the British. His close contemporary Cornelius Steenwyck (2) served as burgomaster of New Amsterdam and later became mayor of New York City under British rule—and one of the city's six wealthiest inhabitants. Young Jacques de Peyster (3), clutching his gold-and-rock-crystal whistle (4), brought from Holland to amuse him, was born into one of the most prominent of Dutch colonial families. In 1664 the English took over New Netherland "without a blow or a tear." The Dutch burghers preferred peaceful surrender to bloodshed and plundering, and accommodated themselves easily enough to the new régime. Captain Johannes Schuyler, shown here with his wife (5), fought the French in early intercolonial wars and later was a peacemaker between the Indians and the English.

3

4

5

33

## The English Takeover

1

With the surrender of New Netherland to the English, King Charles II gave his brother James, duke of York (1), who later became king as James II, a charter for the territory, now named New York. The terms of the surrender had been generous, guaranteeing the Dutch, among other things, full property and inheritance rights. The patroon system of the Dutch, and the extravagant handouts of England's royal governors, brought enormous estates into the hands of certain colonial families. One favored individual, Frederick Philipse, who had come from Holland in 1650 and who for a time had served as Peter Stuyvesant's carpenter, amassed before he died in 1702 holdings of ninety thousand acres, known as Philipsburg Manor (2), over which he ruled like a feudal lord. When James ascended the throne in 1685, he hatched a plan to make New Yorkers subjects of the "Dominion of New England" under Boston-based Governor Edmund Andros (3). But James was ingloriously dethroned in 1688 and Andros was shipped back to London. Robert Hunter (4), who served as governor of New York and New Jersey from 1709 to 1719, was successful in assuaging the rancorous political factionalism that flourished within the colony.

2

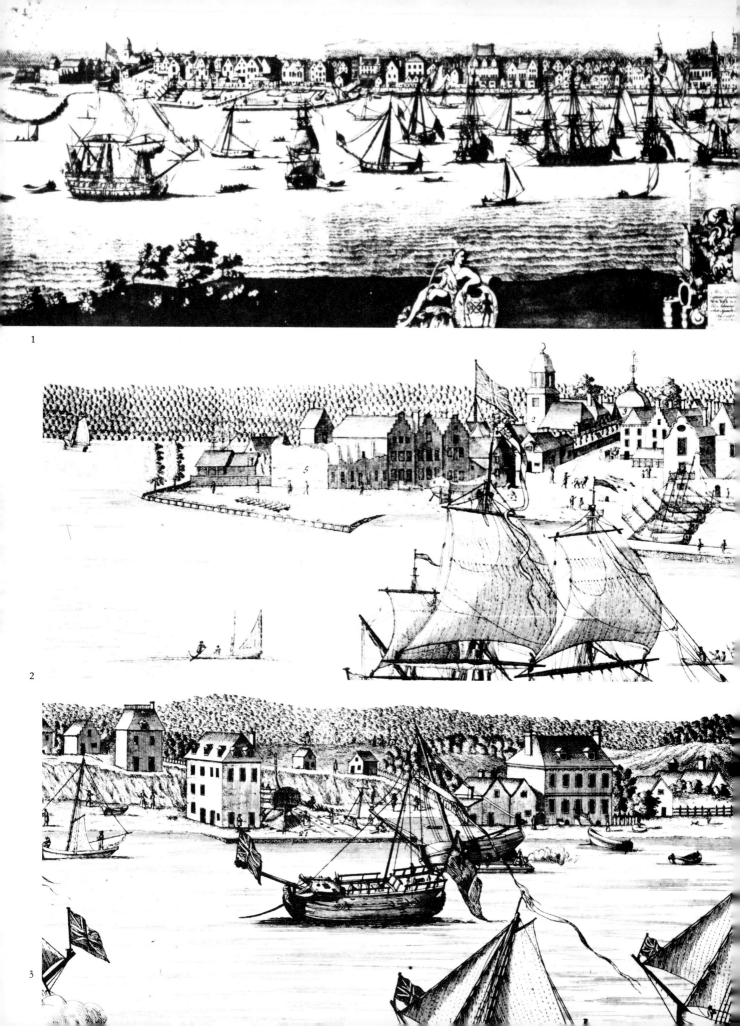

1

2

3

## New York Under English Rule

The most important and detailed view of Manhattan as seen from Brooklyn Heights, with the New Jersey shore of the Hudson shown in the far background, is a six-foot-long panoramic print made from a drawing by William Burgis, engraved about 1717 (1). In it can be traced the development of the city as it pushed northward up the island. At the far left of the scene, the early Dutch buildings of the old city, with their steep roofs and stepped gables (2), contrast with the houses shown farther north on the island, many of them fine mansions overlooking the East River and built in the later, more formal style favored in England at the time (3). Just left of dead center looms the tall spire of the first Trinity Church (4), which had recently been built facing Wall Street and near the new City Hall. In the right foreground (5), cattle and produce from the rural reaches of Brooklyn are being ferried across the East River to be sold in the city. The ferry house, run by James Harding, served as a "publick house of Entertainment" as required by Harding's franchise as ferryman. At the time the population of the city of New York was around seven thousand persons (somewhat less than the population of either Philadelphia or Boston, which were the most important cities in English North America at the time). As ever, New York remained essentially a trading center, its shipyards (6) constantly busy building vessels for the vital West Indies trade. More than two hundred ships cleared the port each year.

Numb. II.

# THE
# New - York Weekly JOURNAL

*Containing the freſheſt Advices, Foreign, and Domeſtick.*

*MUNDAT* November 12, 1733.

Mr. *Zenger.*

INcert the following in your next, and you'll oblige your Friend,
CATO.

*Mira temporum felicitas ubi ſentiri quæ velis, & quæ ſentias dicere licit.*
Tacit.

THE Liberty of the Preſs is a Subject of the greateſt Importance, and in which every Individual is as much concern'd as he is in any other Part of Liberty : therefore it will not be improper to communicate to the Publick the Sentiments of a late excellent Writer upon this Point. ſuch is the Elegance and Perſpicuity of his Writings, ſuch the inimitable Force of his Reaſoning, that it will be difficult to ſay any Thing new that he has not ſaid, or not to ſay that much worſe which he has ſaid.

There are two Sorts of Monarchies, an abſolute and a limited one. In the firſt, the Liberty of the Preſs can never be maintained, it is inconſiſtent with it ; for what abſolute Monarch would ſuffer any Subject to animadvert on his Actions, when it is in his Power to declare the Crime, and to nominate the Puniſhment ? This would make it very dangerous to exerciſe ſuch a Liberty. Beſides the Object againſt which thoſe Pens muſt be directed, is

their Sovereign, the ſole ſupream Magiſtrate ; for there being no Law in thoſe Monarchies, but the Will of the Prince, it makes it neceſſary for his Miniſters to conſult his Pleaſure, before any Thing can be undertaken : He is therefore properly chargeable with the Grievances of his Subjects, and what the Miniſter there acts being in Obedience to the Prince, he ought not to incur the Hatred of the People ; for it would be hard to impute that to him for a Crime, which is the Fruit of his Allegiance, and for refuſing which he might incur the Penalties of Treaſon. Beſides, in an abſolute Monarchy, the Will of the Prince being the Law, a Liberty of the Preſs to complain of Grievances would be complaining againſt the Law, and the Conſtitution, to which they have ſubmitted, or have been obliged to ſubmit ; and therefore, in one Senſe, may be ſaid to deſerve Puniſhment, So that under an abſolute Monarchy, I ſay, ſuch a Liberty is inconſiſtent with the Conſtitution, having no proper Subject in Politics, on which it might be exercis'd, and if exercis'd would incur a certain Penalty.

But in a limited Monarchy, as *England* is, our Laws are known, fixed, and eſtabliſhed. They are the ſtreight Rule and ſure Guide to direct the King, the Miniſters, and other his Subjects : And therefore an Offence againſt the Laws is ſuch an Offence againſt the Conſtitution as ought to receive a proper adequate Puniſhment ; the ſevera
Conſtil

## By his Excellency

*William Cosby*, Captain General and Governour in Chief of the Provinces of *New-York*, *New-Jersey*, and Territories thereon depending in America, Vice-Admiral of the same, and Colonel in His Majesty's Army.

### A PROCLAMATION.

WHereas Ill-minded and Disaffected Persons have lately dispersed in the City of *New-York*, and divers other Places, several Scandalous and Seditious Libels, but more particularly two Printed Scandalous Songs or Ballads, highly defaming the Administration of His Majesty's Government in this Province, tending greatly to inflame the Minds of His Majesty's good Subjects, and to disturb the Publick Peace. And Whereas the Grand Jury for the City and County of New-York did lately, by their Address to me, complain of these Pernicious Practices, and request me to issue a Proclamation for the Discovery of the Offenders, that they might, by Law, receive a Punishment adequate to their Guilt and Crime. I Have therefore thought fit, by and with the Advice of his Majesty's Council, to issue this Proclamation, hereby Promising *Twenty Pounds* as a Reward, to such Person or Persons who shall discover the Author or Authors of the two Scandalous Songs or Ballads aforesaid, to be paid to the Person or Persons discovering the same, as soon as such Author or Authors shall be Convicted of having been the Author or Authors thereof.

*GIVEN under My Hand and Seal at Fort-George in New-York this Sixth Day of November, in the Eighth year of the Reign of Our Sovereign Lord GEORGE the Second, by the Grace of GOD of Great-Britain, France and Ireland, KING, Defender of the Faith, &c. and in the year of Our LORD, 1734.*

*By his Excellency's Command,*
*Fred. Morris, D. Cl. Conc.*

W. COSBY.

### GOD Save the KING

In the summer of 1735, at the corner of Wall and Nassau streets in Manhattan, a trial by jury took place that excited concern and attention not only in New York but in other colonial cities, as well as in London. The *New-York Weekly Journal* (1), a four-page weekly newspaper published by an obscure German immigrant John Zenger, had had the courage and audacity to challenge the ruling governor of the colony, William Cosby (2), for misusing and exceeding the authority of his office. (In setting up his printing shop Zenger had been backed by a faction of local patriots expressly to give voice to such criticisms.) For persisting in his outspoken assertions, Zenger was jailed by Cosby, as the governor's proclamation promised (3), while, one way or another, the *Journal* continued publication of its accusations. Months after his arrest Zenger was brought to trial for his "seditious libel" with little prospect of acquittal. The jury was friendly, but the governor's authority in this matter seemed all but absolute. At the very last moment, when all seemed lost, Andrew Hamilton (4), former attorney general of Philadelphia among other things (he was also one of the architects of Independence Hall), came to Zenger's defense, eloquently pleading for freedom of the press. Ten minutes after he had finished his lengthy discourse, the jury returned a verdict of not guilty. Years later Gouverneur Morris observed that "the trial of Zenger in 1735 was the germ of American freedom, the morning star of that liberty which subsequently revolutionized America."

4

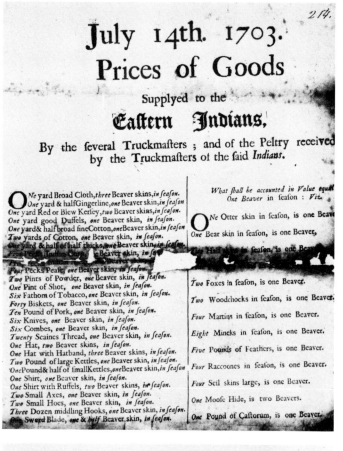

**July 14th. 1703.**
**Prices of Goods**

Supplyed to the

**Eastern Indians,**

By the several Truckmasters ; and of the Peltry received
by the Truckmasters of the said *Indians*.

ONe yard Broad Cloth, *three* Beaver skins, *in season.*
　　One yard & half Gingerline, one Beaver skin, *in season*
One yard Red or Blew Kersey, *two* Beaver skins, *in season.*
One yard good Duffels, one Beaver skin, *in season.*
One yard & half broad fine Cotton, one Beaver skin, *in season*
*Two* yards of Cotton, one Beaver skin, *in season.*
One yard & half of half thicks, one Beaver skin, *in season.*
*Four* Pecks Pease, one Beaver skin, *in season.*
*Two* Pints of Powder, one Beaver skin, *in season.*
One Pint of Shot, one Beaver skin, *in season.*
*Six* Fathom of Tobacco, one Beaver skin, *in season.*
*Forty* Biskets, one Beaver skin, *in season.*
*Ten* Pound of Pork, one Beaver skin, *in season.*
*Six* Knives, one Beaver skin, *in season.*
*Six* Combes, one Beaver skin, *in season.*
*Twenty* Scaines Thread, one Beaver skin, *in season.*
One Hat, *two* Beaver skins, *in season.*
One Hat with Hatband, *three* Beaver skins, *in season.*
*Two* Pound of large Kettles, one Beaver skin, *in season.*
One Pound & half of small Kettles, one Beaver skin, *in season*
One Shirt, one Beaver skin, *in season.*
One Shirt with Ruffels, *two* Beaver skins, *in season.*
*Two* Small Axes, one Beaver skin, *in season.*
*Two* Small Hoes, one Beaver skin, *in season.*
*Three* Dozen middling Hooks, one Beaver skin, *in season.*
One Sword Blade, one & half Beaver skin, *in season.*

What shall be accounted in Value equll
One Beaver in season : *Viz.*

ONe Otter skin in season, is one Beaver.
One Bear skin in season, is one Beaver,
One Half skin in season, is one Beaver.
*Two* Foxes in season, is one Beaver.
*Two* Woodchocks in season, is one Beaver.
*Four* Martins in season, is one Beaver.
*Eight* Mincks in season, is one Beaver.
*Five* Pounds of Feathers, is one Beaver.
*Four* Raccoones in season, is one Beaver.
*Four* Scil skins large, is one Beaver.
One Moose Hide, is *two* Beavers.
One Pound of Castorum, is one Beaver.

T. Grasset S. Sauveur inv. del.　　J. Laroque Sculp.

Indians along the borderlands of New York were inexorably drawn into the vicious circle of trade and strife between the French and English colonists, which centered largely around the vast inland commerce in furs and hides. During much of the colonial period Albany remained an important English focus of this competitive trade. Schedules were printed (1) to establish the value of pelts in terms of the fabrics, clothing, and hardware demanded by the Indians. As one French engraving suggested, the Iroquois were formidable savages to cope with in the northern forests (2). In the winter of 1709–1710 Peter Schuyler (3), first mayor of Albany, sailed for London with five friendly Mohawk sachems to impress them with the might and majesty of Queen Anne and to persuade the English monarch to support Schuyler's bold plans to invade French Canada with the help of Indian allies. (In America the current international conflict involving England and France was known as Queen Anne's War, otherwise remembered as the War of the Spanish Succession.) The sachems, garbed in formal English clothes hastily contrived by a theatrical costumer, were presented to the queen at St. James's Palace. The tall and handsome Thoyanoguen, the so-called King Hendrick, was portrayed thus garbed (4). Thoyanoguen remained a powerful and devoted friend of the English. He and a companion, Etowa Caume, were painted in their forest dress (5, 6). They generally attracted enormous attention in London and were constantly reported in the press. Feted to surfeit and loaded with gifts, four of the kings returned to America in May 1710—one had died en route.

## The French and Indian War

In 1754 the intermittent warfare between the French and English in America broke out into another major conflict. Known here as the French and Indian War, it was to be better known abroad as the Seven Years' War; it was in fact a world war. The Hudson River, Lake George, and Lake Champlain provided a natural route for warring parties of the two antagonists and their indispensable Indian allies (1). In September 1755 the British colonial forces, led by the immigrant New Yorker William Johnson (2) and with support from the Mohawks, defeated a French contingent at Fort William Henry, near Lake George (3). Johnson, a colorful Irishman, was England's resident agent among the Iroquois. He himself had been made a Mohawk sachem and had married a niece of a Mohawk chief. His fortified stone house on the Mohawk River was the scene of numerous Indian councils (4). Johnson had testimonials engraved to present to worthy Indian warriors (5). In the French and Indian War and later, Joseph Brant (Thayendorogea), war chief of the Mohawks, served under Johnson, who sent him to study at a school for Indians in Connecticut. Brant, a devout Christian, later translated the Book of Common Prayer and the Gospel of Mark into the Mohawk language. He continued to fight for the British during the Revolution and, in his waning years, struggled for the rights of his fellow Indians. In 1786 Gilbert Stuart portrayed the great chief in his tribal regalia (6).

5

6

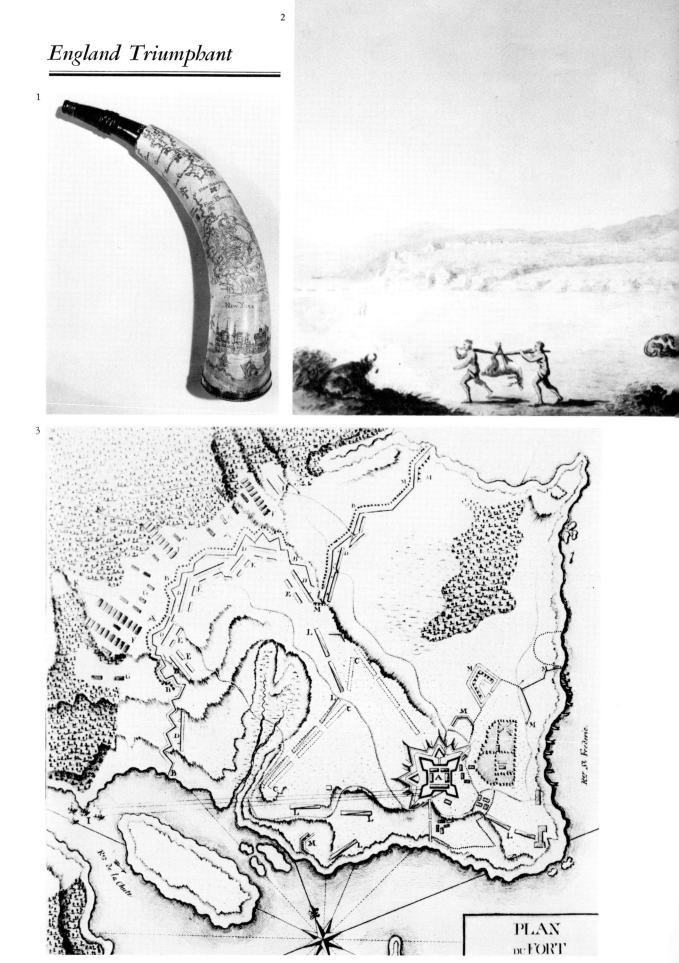

An ingenious engraving on a powder horn made about 1755 depicts the general scene of the French and Indian War in the New York area (1). Fort Ticonderoga, which was to become such a historic American landmark, was built by the French in 1755–1756 to command the passage between Lake George and Lake Champlain (2). Here, on July 8, 1758, after William Pitt in England had ordered the vital bastion taken, one of the most sanguinary battles in British military annals was fought. As can be seen from a contemporary battle map (3), English and colonial troops attacked in an arc from the woods; from their central breastworks around the height, the French met the assault with pointblank musket fire. Almost two thousand of the British force were killed, wounded, or reported missing; the rest retreated. A year later, Major General Jeffrey Amherst, shown here in a portrait by Sir Joshua Reynolds (4), returned to the attack, and this time the French, vastly outnumbered, blew up the fort and abandoned it. Five days later they also pulled out of a fort at Crown Point, fifteen miles to the north, and Amherst temporarily encamped there (5). The central route to Canada was now open to the British. When Quebec fell, later in the year, the issue of the wilderness war was ended.

4

5

## Along City Streets

Probably no city in the United States has so systematically destroyed the physical evidence of its past history as has New York. St. Paul's Chapel, built in 1766 as a virtual duplicate of St. Martin's-in-the-Fields in London, is one of the very few colonial structures to remain standing within metropolitan bounds (1)—an almost miraculous survival in that repeatedly burnt-out and rebuilt city. Fires menaced the community from the start. A fire department was authorized in 1737 and by 1750 the city had six engines. The accompanying detail from a notice of the Hand-in-Hand Fire Company (2) shows the customary bucket brigade passing water to the engine from a neighboring hand pump, while people carry away salvage from the burning building in sacks and baskets. In 1817, to preserve a record of what the city had been like in 1768, Joseph B. Smith painted a view of John Street between William and Nassau streets (3). The first Methodist church building erected in America, Wesley's Chapel, is shown in the center of the painting. Most of the figures are portraits of actual persons, done from memory (4). One of the men standing before the chapel, Captain Thomas Webb, a disciple of Wesley (5), wears a patch over the eye he lost during the French and Indian War.

3

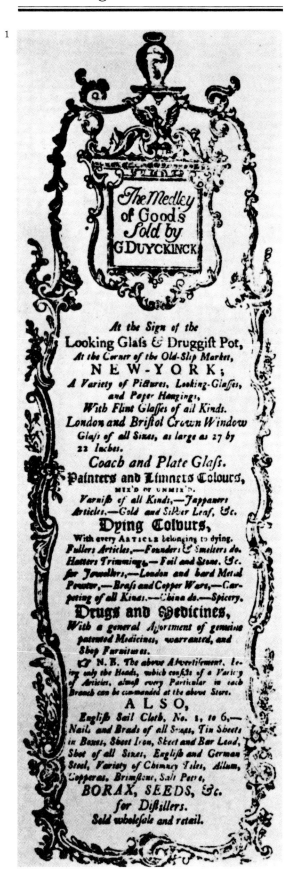

Newspaper advertising showed the variety of New York's trade and industry. In 1769 the *New-York Gazette* and the *Weekly Post-Boy* carried an elaborately framed announcement by G. Duyckinck, a merchant who offered for sale just about everything from pictures and window glass to patent medicines and brimstone (1). In Albany, James Chestney was prepared to make chairs "to any pattern on the shortest notice"—slat-backs, Windsors, and splat-backs in the Hudson Valley style, as the illustration in his advertisement in the *Albany Gazette* indicates (2). That same paper carried a notice by Nehemiah Bassett that he would supply warranted watches and clocks that he made himself or imported, and that he would repair time-keeping instruments "in the best manner and on the most reasonable terms" (3). In 1765 H. Gaine was prepared to pay "ready money for clean linen rags" that he could use in his New York paper manufactory (4). He even offered a premium to the person delivering "the greatest quantity of good clean dry linen rags" in that year. The year before, W. Hawxhurst appealed for laborers to man his iron manufactory on Sterling Mountain (5). He offered his anchors and wagon tires for sale for cash or "Connecticut Proclamation bills." A society organized for protection and improvement of workmen was formed as early as 1747. In 1767 a "friendly society of tradesmen, house carpenters, in the City of New-York" was established with articles and regulations that in its broadside (6) carefully detailed the rules to which its members must subscribe and noted penalties which they must pay for cursing, becoming "disgulfed in Liquor," and similar offenses against decorum during their periodic meetings.

## 1

# Living in Style

New York emerged from the French and Indian War fat with profits made on government contracts, shipping, and privateering. In the years immediately following, hundreds of thousands of pounds of New York money went into the construction and furbishing of mansions and estates, and into "French and Spanish wines, portrait painting, carriages from London." Between 1765 and 1768 Stephen Van Rensselaer II, seventh patroon of the manor of Rensselaerwyck, built one of the most elegant houses in the colonies. Hand-painted wallpaper made to order and measure in London, decorated with adaptations of contemporary European paintings, lined the great central hall (1), now reinstalled in the Metropolitan Museum. An unidentified gentleman had the artist John Mare paint his portrait with his hand resting on a chair made in New York in the fashionable Chippendale style (2). Gaming tables were made for those with time to spare and money to wager (3). James Beekman enjoyed a French coach with his coat of arms painted on the door panels (4). During a visit to New York in 1774 John Adams was much impressed by such "Opulence and Splendor" as he saw there. It was by no means all new money. Early in the century Lewis Morris, first lord of the manor of Morrisania and associate of Governor Robert Hunter, sailed about the New York waterways in his private yacht (5); and his son and namesake, who owned one of the finest stables in New York, treasured a silver bowl celebrating his racing horse Old Tenor (6).

6

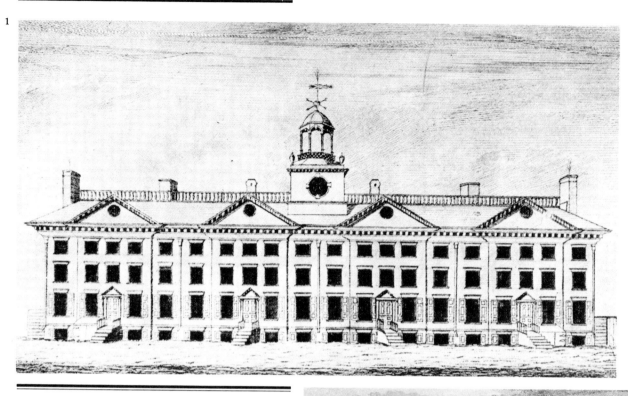

1

In the year 1754, coinciding with the outbreak of the French and Indian War, New York's cultural and intellectual life was enriched by the founding of two enduring institutions: King's College, later to become Columbia University, and the New York Society Library, the oldest library in the city. The original college building (1) also can be seen in the distance in a view of lower Manhattan drawn in 1763—with an incongruous palm tree in the foreground (2). The name of Samuel Verplanck, a fifth-generation descendant of early Dutch settlers, is listed with the first graduating class (3). In 1771 Verplanck had his likeness painted by John Singleton Copley (4), when that prominent Boston artist visited New York. Copley reported that the New York gentry were so discerning he could "slight nothing" in painting their portraits. An early bookplate of the New York Society Library symbolically suggests its educational endeavors (5). (Samuel Verplanck was a trustee of the library.) The Society still actively serves the New York "gentry" and others with its exceptional collections, which incorporate the library early formed in Boston by John Winthrop.

2

52

# CATALOGUS

Eorum exhibens Nomina qui in COLLEGIO REGALI, NOVI-EBORACI, Laurea alicujus Gradus donati fuerunt, ab anno 1758 ad annum 1774.

NEW-YORK: PRINTED BY H. GAINE, AT HIS PRINTING-OFFICE IN HANOVER-SQUARE.

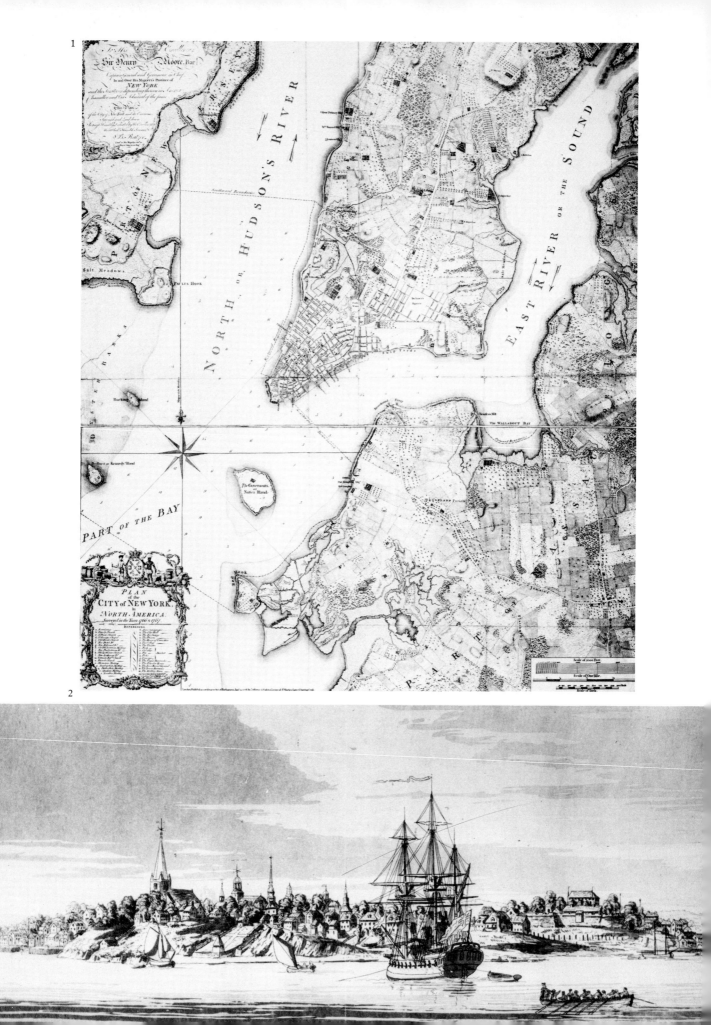

# On the Eve of War

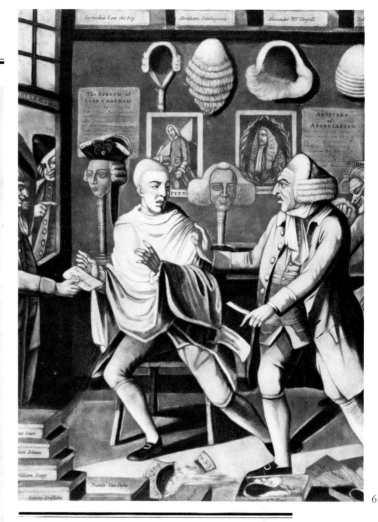

3

## To the PUBLIC.

THE Senfe of the City relative to the Landing the India Company's Tea, being fignified to Captain Lockyer, by the Committee, neverthelefs, it is the Defire of a Number of the Citizens, that at his Departure from hence, he fhould fee, with his own Eyes, their Deteftation of the Meafures purfued by the Miniftry and the India Company, to enflave this Country. This will be declared by the Convention of the People at his Departure from this City; which will be on next Saturday Morning, about nine o'Clock, when no Doubt, every Friend to this Country will attend. The Bells will give the Notice about an Hour before he embarks from Murray's Wharf.

By Order of the COMMITTEE.

NEW YORK, APRIL 21ft, 1774.

4

## ADVERTISEMENT.

THE Committee of Correfpondence in New-York, having on Monday Night laft proceeded to the Nomination of five Perfons to go as Delegates for the faid City and County, on the propofed General Congrefs at Philadelphia, on the 1ft of September next; the five following Perfons were nominated for that Purpofe,

Philip Livingfton,
James Duane,
John Alfop,
John Jay,
Ifaac Low.

The Inhabitants, therefore, of this City and County, are requefted to meet at the City-Hall, on THURSDAY next, at 12 o'Clock, in order to approve of the faid five Perfons as Delegates, or to choofe fuch other in their Stead, as to their Wifdom fhall feem meet.

By Order of the Committee,

ISAAC LOW, CHAIRMAN.

TUESDAY, 5th July, 1774.

5

## IN PROVINCIAL CONGRESS,

NEW-YORK, JUNE 13, 1776.

WHEREAS this Congrefs have been informed by the Continental Congrefs, and have great Reafon to believe that an Invafion of this Colony will very fhortly be made.

RESOLVED UNANIMOUSLY, That it be, and it is hereby recommended to all the Officers in the Militia in this Colony, forthwith to review the fame, and give Orders that they prepare themfelves, and be ready to march whenever they may be called upon.

ORDERED, That the aforegoing Refolution be publifhed in the public News-Papers, and printed in Hand-Bills to be diftributed.

Extract from the Minutes,

ROBERT BENSON, Sec'ry.

An accurate plan of the city of New York and vicinity (1), drawn by a lieutenant of the Royal American Regiment and published early in 1776, shows the spacious harbor and interlocking waterways (reaching far north into Canada) that made the port a primary objective of British military strategy with the approach of the Revolution. A skyline view of Manhattan Island seen from the northwest (2), also issued shortly before the signing of the Declaration of Independence, was prepared for the use of the Royal Navy. At the time the population of the city was about 23,500 persons. Many of those residents were loyal to the Crown; New York would provide more troops for George III than for George Washington. Among the public announcements that heralded the impending hostilities were: a notice, issued soon after the Boston Tea Party, urging a boycott of tea (3); a list of proposed delegates to the Continental Congress (4); and a call for troops to resist a British invasion of New York (5). One of many popular English prints that reflected pro-American sentiments (6) pictured a New York barber refusing to complete shaving the captain of a British troop ship upon learning his identity.

## *Preparation for a Siege*

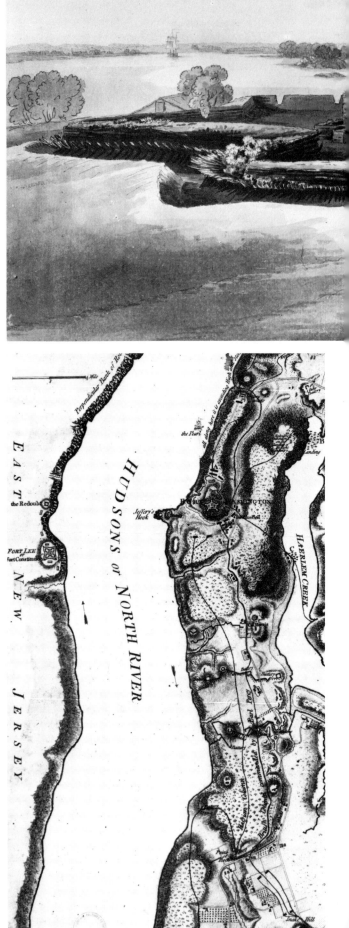

In April 1776, immediately after he had forced the British to evacuate Boston, George Washington (1) marched his little army to New York to prepare for a fresh campaign centered at that point. The fortification of New York had begun before Washington's arrival; a sketch by a British engineer shows the nine-gun battery at Horn's Hook (2), near what is now Eighty-ninth Street and East End Avenue. At the northern tip of Manhattan Island, opposite a flanking battery on the New Jersey side of the Hudson River, Fort Washington was designed to prevent British ships from forcing a passage to the north (3). Shortly after Washington's appearance on the scene, the largest expeditionary force ever assembled by Great Britain arrived at New York Harbor. About two hundred vessels, a number of which can be seen lying off Staten Island in a contemporary drawing (4), carried more than thirty thousand trained professional soldiers under the command of Sir William Howe (5). Very shortly after its arrival, the British fleet revealed the ineffectiveness of the American shore batteries when two freighters, the *Phoenix* and the *Rose,* blithely sailed thirty miles up the Hudson, passing Fort Washington without trouble. About a month later the two vessels safely made the return trip, although American fire ships (6) attempted to destroy them.

4

5

6

1

2

In his efforts to defend New York, Washington was both outmanned and outmaneuvered. The American troops were forced to retreat from Long Island to Manhattan and thence north out of the area altogether. The crucial British attack on Fort Washington was launched from three directions, as pictured in an eyewitness watercolor by Thomas Davies, a British officer (1): Hessians attacked the fort directly (partly visible on the high ground at center); British troops (in the foreground) assaulted the fort's outposts from the Harlem River; and the British frigate *Pearl* shelled American positions from the Hudson River (right background). Meanwhile, another British force, under General Cornwallis, scaled the Palisades opposite Yonkers and forced the American garrison to abandon Fort Lee (2). The battle for Manhattan was won. Washington made the last stand of the campaign at White Plains, where he was again defeated on October 28, 1776 (3). But once again he saved the bulk of his troops and with them retreated to New Jersey to anticipate Howe's next move. John Trumbull depicted the sorry plight of some American prisoners of war, jailed in a rotting British hulk anchored off the Brooklyn shore (4). During Washington's withdrawal from New York, on September 21, a large part of the city was destroyed by fire. Trinity Church, among almost five hundred other structures, was reduced to ashes (5).

Sir Joshua Reynolds's portrait of Major General John Burgoyne (1) suggests the flamboyance of the soldier who wagered at London's very fashionable Brooks's Club that he would win the war in America and return home victorious by Christmas Day, 1777. Burgoyne planned to lead an army of British, American Tory, Hessian, and Indian troops down from Canada past Lake Champlain, Fort Ticonderoga, and Lake George to Albany. There he would be met by another force, under Brigadier General Barry St. Leger, sweeping from the west along the Mohawk Valley, and a third army, under Howe, coming up from New York, thus cutting off New England from the other colonies and disconcerting whatever other strategy Washington had in mind. Burgoyne enjoined his Indian allies to wage war in a civilized fashion (2), soon after he had headed south into New York from a staging area at St. John's on the Richelieu River (3). But his command had little effect. The killing and scalping of Jane McCrea as she awaited her fiancé, a British officer, was but one horrifying incident of the campaign (4). Burgoyne's army passed down Lake Champlain (5) and took Fort Ticonderoga without a struggle. But then his serious trouble began.

4

5

# *The Battle of Saratoga*

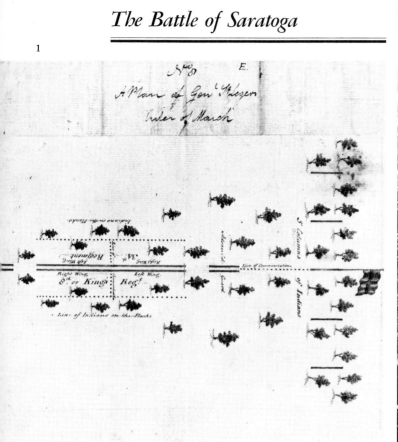

## 2

Howe's orders to join Burgoyne arrived after he had already decided to move toward Philadelphia, and he never headed north to Albany. The dashing Barry St. Leger, who was to join Burgoyne from the west, also failed to reach Albany. His troops, mauled by colonial resistance and then by his own panicking Indian allies, never could follow the order of march (1) that was later found in his hastily abandoned writing desk. Deprived of support and suffering successive defeats as he tried to force his way to Albany through American lines, Burgoyne withdrew the fragments of his army to an encampment on the west side of the Hudson (2). Assailed from every side, he attempted a retreat to Ticonderoga; but near the little village of Saratoga, surrounded and outnumbered three to one, more than five thousand crack British and German troops laid down their arms on October 17, 1777 (3). Major General Horatio Gates (4) claimed credit for the victory which, incomprehensibly, he neglected to report to Washington. A few months after the report of that conclusive victory reached Europe, France officially recognized the new republic and signed a treaty pledging its full military support—a development duly recorded in an English cartoon showing "The Horse America Throwing His Master" and thereby attracting the French alliance (5).

4

5

# Arnold and André

PLAN
des Forts, Batteries
et Poste de West-Point.
1780.

A. Magasin détruit.
B. Vieilles Casernes.
C. Magasin militaire.
D. Muraille.
E. Embarcaderes.
F. Hôpital.
G. Batteries.
H. Horn-Point.
I. Colline de Bun
K. Duck-Point.
L. Jardin de Kos
M. Prisons. Caser
N. Ecole du Génie
O. Attcliers.
P. Etang.
R. Magasin mili
S. Bibliothèque.
T. Quartier-Général.
U. Laboratoire.

The towering rocky mass on the west bank of the Hudson River, about fifty miles north of New York City, a fortified site known as West Point (1), was a vital key to American defenses. As shown on a contemporary map (2), a heavy iron chain forged in a nearby ironworks stretched across the river to block passage upstream; cannon bristled on the heights. In 1780, with the British still occupying Manhattan, General Benedict Arnold (3) was, at his own request, given command of that critical post. After heroic exploits at Saratoga and elsewhere, Arnold had become embittered by what he considered insufficient appreciation of his worth by Congress, and he decided to sell out to the British for an "ample" cash return. But his plan to betray West Point was discovered when the young British spy, Major John André, was captured with incriminating documents on his person (4). André's self-portrait (5) was made the day before he was hanged at Washington's headquarters at Tappan, New York. Arnold escaped and served for a time with the British Army. His effigy—two-faced, as befits a traitor—was paraded through the streets of Philadelphia (6) by American patriots.

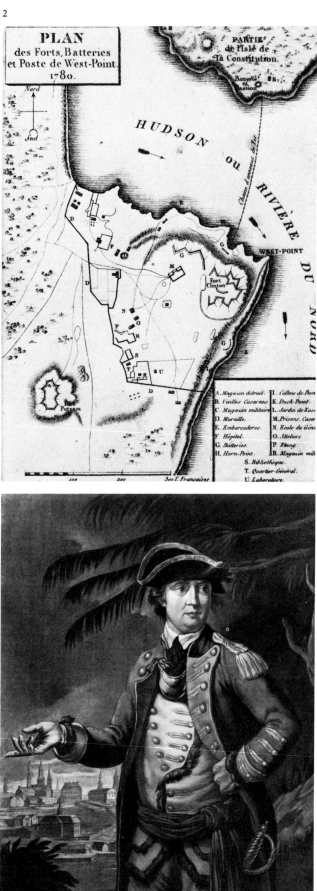

## Frontier Warfare

In western New York savage border warfare continued with British Loyalists and Indians fighting the settlers along the Mohawk Valley (1)—and large landholders fighting small farmers. All too often the bloodshed had little to do with the basic issues of colonists' rights that had launched the Revolution. Just before the war, Benjamin West in London portrayed the Loyalist superintendent of Indian Affairs, Colonel Guy Johnson, with his Mohawk ally Chief Joseph Brant (2), who directed raids against patriotic settlements. Even the British were appalled by the barbarism that was reported. One London cartoon shows George III sharing human flesh cannibal-style with his Indian allies (3). To put an end to the gory frontier massacres and to protect his own position along the Hudson, Washington in the spring of 1779 ordered a vigorous campaign through Indian lands (4); it was led by such outstanding patriotic leaders as Generals John Sullivan (6) and James Clinton. From 1780 Colonel Marinus Willet, a hero of other, earlier campaigns (5), commanded New York troops in the Mohawk Valley, and shortly after Cornwallis's surrender at Yorktown, the Tory and Indian menace in the state was broken for good.

3

4

5                                          6

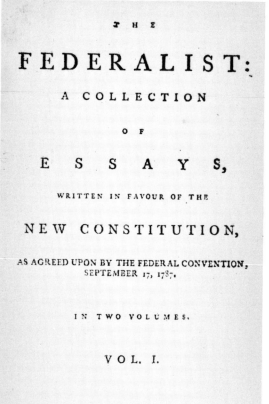

THE

# FEDERALIST:

A COLLECTION

OF

ESSAYS,

WRITTEN IN FAVOUR OF THE

NEW CONSTITUTION,

AS AGREED UPON BY THE FEDERAL CONVENTION,
SEPTEMBER 17, 1787.

IN TWO VOLUMES.

VOL. I.

NEW-YORK:

PRINTED AND SOLD BY J. AND A. M'LEAN.
No. 41, HANOVER-SQUARE.
M,DCC,LXXXVIII.

During the bitter struggle over the ratification of the federal Constitution, more than a few New Yorkers believed that their state might better do it alone as a separate and independent commonwealth. Others felt as strongly that if New York did not join the Union of its own accord, it would have to be brought in by force. That New York did ratify was due in good measure to the persuasive and skilled arguments written by Alexander Hamilton (1) and John Jay (2)—with James Madison of Virginia—which appeared in the newspapers under the byline "Publius." These essays, quickly republished in book form as *The Federalist* (3), remain extraordinarily brilliant commentaries on the Constitution. It became evident that without New York the Union would be hopelessly divided, and that apart from the Union, New York would be isolated. On July 26, 1788, ratification was voted. Confident supporters in New York City celebrated the occasion three days early with a federal procession in which, along with other groups of artisans, the Society of Pewterers marched under their silk banner (4). At an official banquet pavilion (5), erected to celebrate the occasion, a crowd of six thousand feasted and heard speeches. Jay became the first Chief Justice of the Supreme Court when the Constitution was adopted, and later served as governor of New York. Hamilton met his death in a duel with Aaron Burr in 1804.

4

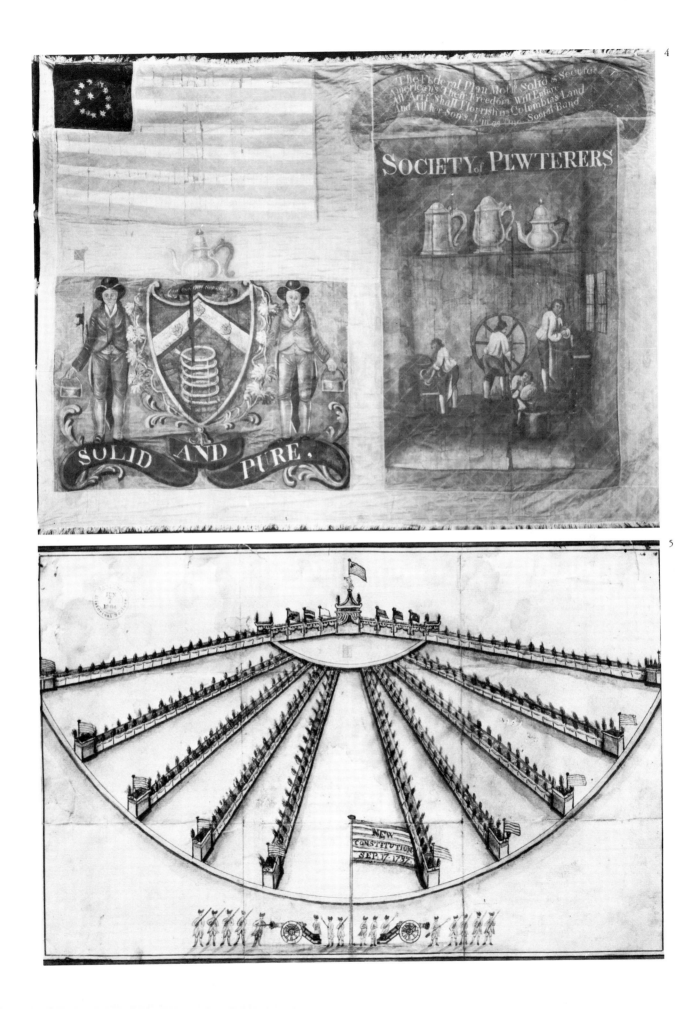

## Capital of the Nation

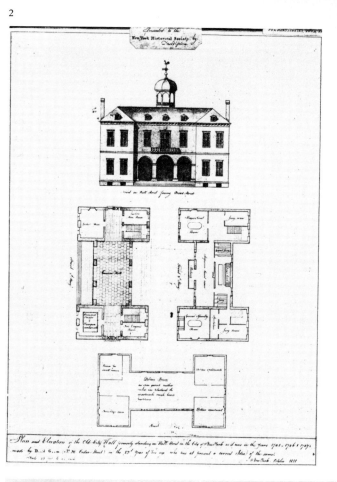

George Washington was inaugurated as the nation's first President in New York City on April 30, 1789 (1). In anticipation of the city's being chosen as capital, the old City Hall—the city's second, built around 1700—had been especially modernized to accommodate the national government (2). The conversion of the ancient structure, and the design of a suitable chamber in which the House of Representatives could meet (3), was entrusted to Pierre Charles L'Enfant, a French veteran of the American Revolution. (L'Enfant had designed the pavilion shown on the preceding page and a few years later drew up plans for the new federal city of Washington, D.C.) The inaugural ceremony attracted people from all over. "The windows and roofs of the houses were crowded," reported one observer, "and in the streets the throng was so dense that it seemed as if one might literally walk on the heads of the people." When the capital was moved to Philadelphia the next year, it was gloomily predicted that New York would be deserted and revert to a wilderness. Federal Hall, on Wall Street at the head of Broad, once again became City Hall, with seventeenth-century Dutch buildings among its more picturesque neighbors (4). The grateful citizens of New York had offered L'Enfant ten acres of Manhattan real estate as a gift, but this he declined, feeling he had no need to stoop to "petty gains."

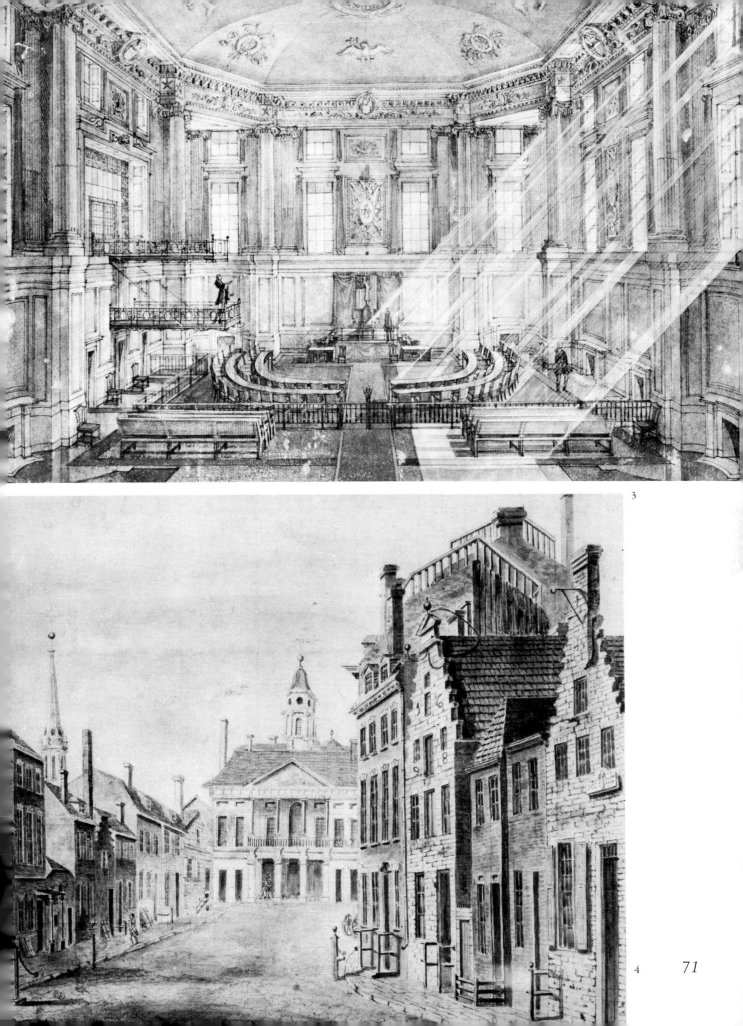

## Return to the Sea

Early in the history of the new nation it was reported that New York City enjoyed "the most eligible situation for commerce in the United States." The ink was hardly dry on the treaty that formally ended the Revolution when a former privateer of the war days, the *Empress of China*, set sail from New York for Canton to open direct trade with the Orient. A likeness of this pioneering vessel as it lay at anchor in the Far East was painted on a Chinese fan (1) that was presented to the ship's captain by Cantonese officials. The ship's successful return to her home port was reported in the *Pennsylvania Packet* for May 16, 1785 (2). One testimonial of the flourishing trade that followed is a huge porcelain punch bowl decorated with the seals of the United States and of the city of New York, with varied scenes, and the legend, recording the fact that the bowl was made in Canton (3). It was presented to the corporation of the city on July 4, 1812. By 1797 the port of New York was handling more foreign trade than Philadelphia, still the nation's largest city. The arrival and clearance of every ship was registered at the Tontine Coffee House, at the corner of Wall and Water streets (4), where merchants, brokers, and others met to do business "in a large way." At the same time, one could have walked beyond Wall Street and almost immediately encountered a rural scene (5).

NEW-YORK, May 12.

We have the satisfaction of announcing the val of the ship *Empress of China*, captain G from the EAST-INDIES, at this port, yesterday ter a voyage of 14 months and 24 days. She from this port about the 15th of February, and arrived at Canton in August, having touch the Cape de Verdes—she took her departure China the first of last January, and in return to at the Cape of Good Hope, from whence the her passage here in about two months.—The during this long voyage have been remarkable thy. The carpenter, who went out in a bad health, died on the homeward passage.

We learn that captain Greene met with usage during his stay in Canton—the British modore was the first who saluted his flag on his val here.

As the ship has returned with a full cargo, such articles as we generally import from Euro correspondent observes, that it presages a happy period of our being able to dispense with burdensome and unnecessary traffick, which b fore we have carried on with Europe—to the prejudice of our rising empire, and future prospects of solid greatness: And that whet not, the ship's cargo be productive of those a tages to the owners, which their merits for th dertaking deserve, he conceives it will prome welfare of the United States in general, by in their citizens with emulation to equal, if no their mercantile rivals.

Some years ago, when the advantages of tra navigation were better studied and more value they are now, the arrival of a vessel after so p ous a voyage, from so distant a part of our

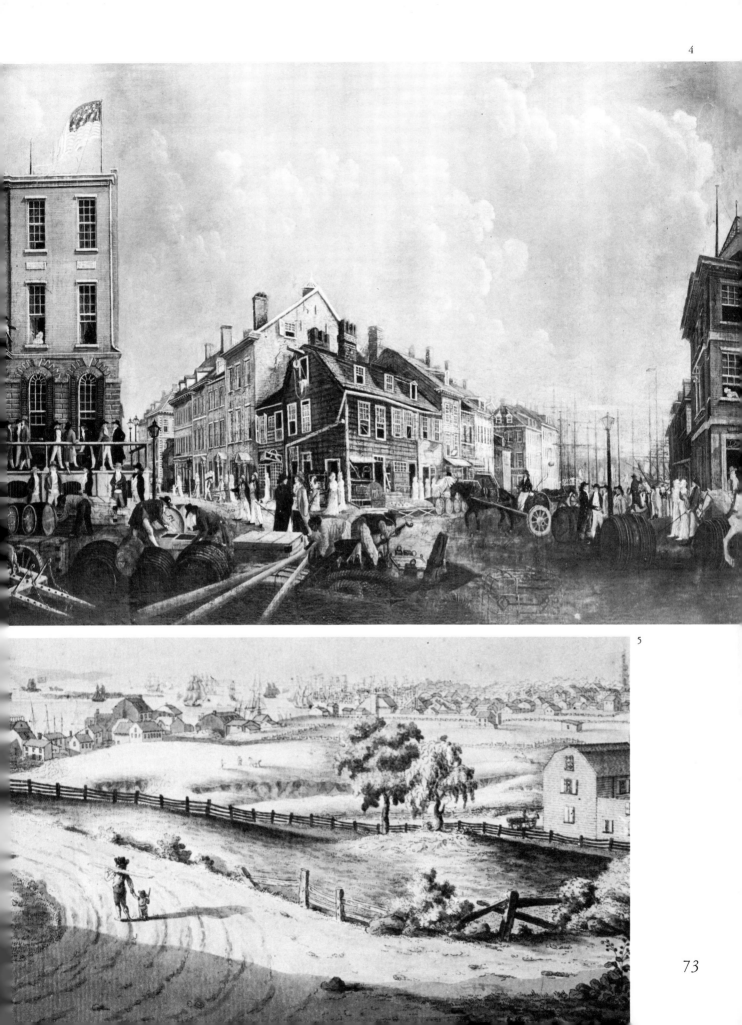

During the first three years that John Jay was governor, he occupied the government house in New York City (1), a handsome structure that was leased as a boardinghouse after the state capital was moved to Albany in 1797. At that time Albany was a village of just 863 houses, with a strong impress from its Dutch origins that lingered well into the next century (2). Across the East River from Manhattan, Brooklyn kept its separate identity (it did not become a part of New York City until 1898). A winter view of Brooklyn streets painted about 1817–1820 by Francis Guy, an eccentric English cloth dyer, recalls Pieter Brueghel's paintings of peasant life in Holland more than two centuries earlier (3). On Manhattan, New York's third City Hall was started in 1803 and first occupied in 1811. The marble building, which still serves its original purpose, was the joint effort of a native-born architect-builder, John McComb, Jr., and a French architect, Joseph François Mangin. A Swedish artist visiting America, Baron Alex Klinckowstrom, pictured the building in 1819 as it appeared from Broadway (4). "You will get a good idea of this part of New York, which is really attractive," he wrote of his sketch, ". . . you will see the costumes in use here, and also all the vehicles, from the elegant coach down to the modest pushcart, on which the licensed porter is busily transferring the traveller's belongings to the harbour." In the foreground of his scene on Broadway he included one of the scavenger pigs, upon whose meandering rooting the disposal of the city's refuse largely depended.

4

# *Urban Developments*

## 7

As in all the other growing cities of the new nation, life in New York encountered developing urban problems that required some invention and collective effort to cope with adequately. In the twenty years following the Revolution, the city's police force increased about five times, although it consisted largely of constables, or marshals, on call during the day. At night the City Watch, a lonely "moonlighter" identified by his stick and leather hat, patroled the dimly lit streets (1). Firefighting was in the hands of volunteers who manned the bucket brigades that fed water to primitive, hand-operated pumping machines (2). Wild dogs, a menace to the public since Dutch days, were rounded up by a hired dogkiller (3). Six public markets, including the Fly Market at Maiden Lane and Pearl Street (4), served to provision the increasing population; their function was supplemented by bakers (5), buttermilk peddlers (6), water purveyors (7), and other vendors who carted their offerings along the cobbled streets. One Potpye Palmer with his garbage cart and bell (8) hauled away the refuse. Such was the passing scene around 1810 when William Chappel painted the pictures on these pages.

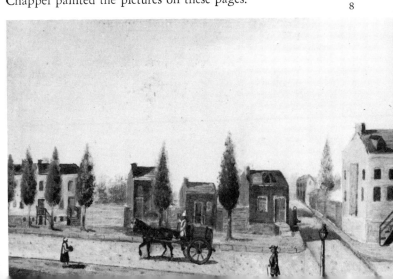

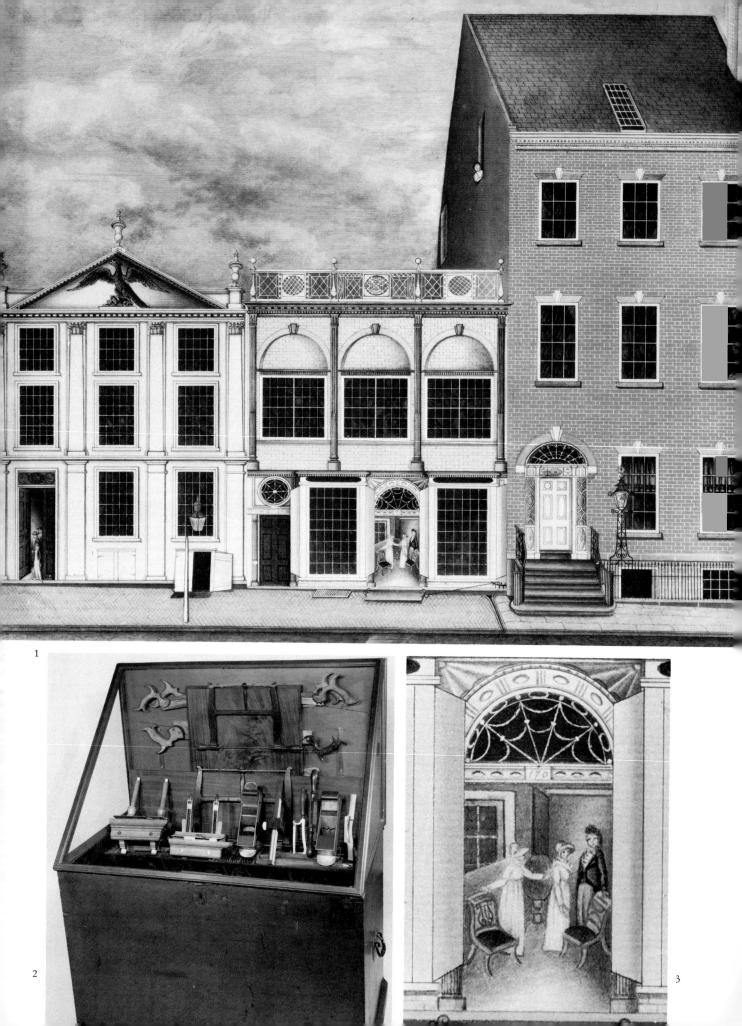

## 8

1

2

3

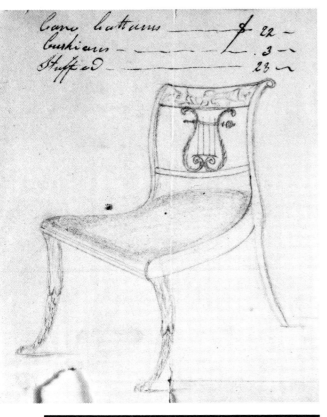

Very shortly after the Revolution Duncan Phyfe came to America from his native Scotland and, following a brief period in Albany, settled in New York City, where he soon became known as one of the city's most talented craftsmen. His furniture shop and warehouse (1), which stood on Fulton Street, has long since disappeared, but his tool chest has happily survived (2). Phyfe's creative abilities profoundly influenced contemporary furniture design in and about the metropolis. In the accompanying drawing of his shop a detail of the salesroom (3) shows chairs that resemble one represented in a sketch attributed to Phyfe (4) and corresponding to a surviving example (5) that is associated with his name. When he died in 1854 at the age of eighty-six, Phyfe left an estate valued at almost half a million dollars. Most craftsmen of the time were in fact budding capitalists who, following their apprenticeships, hoped to work for themselves soon. Labor problems were minimal. However, to protect themselves and their families, the city's journeymen of various trades had from an early date formed labor organizations; the membership certificate for one such association is shown at right (6). During the first decade of the nineteenth century twenty-four such societies were incorporated in New York alone.

## The Federal Style

After the Revolution New York enjoyed a state-wide housing boom. Shortly after 1800 States Morris Dyckman built an elegant twenty-room mansion in Westchester County in the new federal style, a house named Boscobel that, as a model of classic grace, has no counterpart in the nation (1). It was moved to a site on the Hudson in Garrison, New York, and opened to the public in 1961. At Delhi in Delaware County, Judge Gideon Frisbee built his home in the new fashion (2) in 1804, on the site of an earlier log cabin where the first county court had met in 1797. In 1810 Stephen Jumel bought the old summer home of the loyalist Roger Morris on Manhattan Island, which had served as Washington's headquarters during the Battle of Harlem Heights, and then remodeled it in the classical style (3). The father-in-law of William H. Seward, Lincoln's Secretary of State and founder of the Republican party, raised a house in this federal fashion at Auburn, New York, in 1816 (4); it subsequently became Seward's home. James Fenimore Cooper's father built his home, Otsego Hall, at Cooperstown, in the federal style. In 1816 the novelist's mother was portrayed seated in the large entrance chamber of the building (5). With the advice of his friend, the artist-inventor Samuel F. B. Morse, the author in 1834 remodeled the house in the Gothic revival style (6). The house was destroyed by fire in 1853.

1

2

3

## The Scientific Spirit

America's first scientific expedition was launched in 1801 on a farm in Ulster County, New York, by the versatile artist, handicraftsman, and Revolutionary War veteran Charles Willson Peale. With financial aid from the American Philosophical Society (then headed by his friend Thomas Jefferson) and with equipment supplied by the army and navy, Peale dug from a bog on that site the bones of a mastodon—a discovery he memorialized in one of his most engaging paintings (1). Subsequently he reassembled the skeleton for exhibition in his Philadelphia museum. The same year as Peale's dig, Dr. David Hosack (2), professor of botany at Columbia College, founded the Elgin Botanic Garden in New York City (3) on the site where Rockefeller Center now stands. Here he assembled a large collection of native and exotic plants, trees, and shrubs helpful in his teaching and research. Hosack was also a physician at the New York Hospital (4), undertaken by private subscription and chartered in 1771 but not finally ready for use until 1791. (The original building was destroyed by fire and, when reconstructed, served as a barracks for troops during the Revolution.) The polyglot nature of New York's population is evident in a chart in the hospital's annual report for 1797 (5), indicating that the patients admitted that year were natives of seventeen different countries.

### Nº I.

## Charity Extended To All.

STATE of the *New-York Hospital* for the Year 1797.

Account of the Number of Patients admitted in the New-York Hospital, from 31st January, 1797, to 31st January, 1798.

| DISEASES. | Remaining from 1796 | Admitted from Jan. 1797 | Total | Cured | Relieved | Discharged by desire | Eloped and disorderly | Died | Remaining |
|---|---|---|---|---|---|---|---|---|---|
| Amenorrhea, | | 4 | | 2 | | 2 | | | |
| Atrophia, | 1 | | 1 | | | | | | 1 |
| Ascites, | 1 | 15 | 16 | 9 | 3 | | 1 | 3 | |
| Burns, | 1 | 3 | 4 | 3 | | | | | 1 |
| Cancers, | | 1 | 2 | 1 | 1 | | | | |
| Diarrhœa, | 1 | 7 | 8 | 5 | 1 | | | | 2 |
| Febris Intermit, | 3 | 37 | 40 | 27 | | | 3 | 9 | 1 |
| Frozen Limbs, | 12 | 19 | 31 | 13 | 2 | 5 | | 2 | 9 |
| Fractures, | 5 | 16 | 21 | 9 | 3 | | | 2 | 7 |
| Gonorrhœa, | 1 | 6 | 7 | 3 | | | 2 | 2 | |
| Mania, | 4 | 18 | 22 | 4 | 5 | 1 | 1 | 2 | 9 |
| Melancholia, | 1 | | 1 | | | | | | 1 |
| Ophthalmia, | 1 | 5 | 6 | 3 | | | 1 | | 2 |
| Palfy, | 1 | 2 | 3 | 1 | | | | | 1 |
| Phlem, | 1 | | 1 | 1 | | | | | |
| Pthifis Pulmon. | 1 | 5 | 6 | | 2 | 1 | | 3 | |
| Pneumonia, | 11 | 48 | 59 | 24 | | 2 | | 13 | 20 |
| Rachitis, | 1 | | 1 | 1 | | | | | |
| Rheumatifm, | 5 | 37 | 42 | 24 | 9 | | 4 | 1 | 4 |
| Schrophula, | 2 | 3 | 5 | 3 | | | | 1 | 1 |
| Syphilis, | 24 | 103 | 127 | 76 | 15 | 1 | 11 | 1 | 23 |
| Tumor, | 1 | 2 | 3 | 2 | | | | | 1 |
| Ulcers, | 21 | 68 | 89 | 39 | 10 | 1 | 13 | 3 | 23 |
| Wounds, | 5 | 13 | 18 | 15 | 2 | | | | 1 |
| Apoplexy, | | 2 | 2 | | | | | 2 | |
| Anafarca, | | 6 | 6 | | | | | 5 | 1 |
| Afthma, | | 1 | 1 | | | | | 1 | |
| Colica, | | 2 | 2 | 1 | | | | 1 | |
| Cataract, | | 2 | 2 | 2 | | | | | |
| Catarrh, | | 1 | 1 | 1 | | | | | |
| Dilocations, | | 2 | 2 | 2 | | | | | |
| Dyfenteria, | | 5 | 5 | 3 | 1 | | | | 1 |
| Dyfpepfia, | | 5 | 5 | | 1 | | | 2 | 2 |
| Fiftula, | | 4 | 4 | 1 | 1 | | | 1 | 1 |
| Gravel, | | 2 | 2 | 2 | | | | | |
| Hemoptifis, | | 1 | 1 | 1 | | | | | |
| Herpes, | | 2 | 2 | 2 | | | | | |
| Hepatitis, | | 2 | 2 | 1 | | | 1 | | |
| Luxation, | | 9 | 9 | 9 | | | | | |
| Lumbar Abfcefs, | | 2 | 2 | | | | | 1 | |
| Sciatica, | | 1 | 1 | 1 | | | | | |
| Scorbutus, | | 1 | 1 | | | | 1 | | |
| Tinea Capitis, | | 1 | 1 | 1 | | | | | |
| Typhus, | | 8 | 8 | 5 | 1 | | | 2 | |
| White Swelling, | | 1 | 1 | | | | | | |
| | 106 | 472 | 578 | 206 | 60 | 12 | 41 | 57 | 112 |

RECAPITULATION.

Patients Remaining in the Hospital 31st January, 1797, — 106
Admitted from the 31st January, 1797, to 31st January, 1798, — 472 — 578
Dif charged.—Cured, — 206
Relieved, — 62
By Defire, — 12
Diforderly and Eloped, — 41
Died, — 57 — 466

Remaining in the Hospital 31st January, 1798, — 112

—Who were Natives of the following Places,—

| America. | England. | Scotland. | Ireland. | France. | Germany. | Spain. | Ruffia. | Portugal. | Sweden. | Holland. | Denmark. | Italy. | Norway. | Africa. | Eaft-Indies. | Weft-Indies. | TOTAL. |
|---|---|---|---|---|---|---|---|---|---|---|---|---|---|---|---|---|---|
| 245 | 37 | 23 | 163 | 9 | 15 | 8 | 2 | 1 | 7 | 11 | 3 | 3 | 3 | 8 | 8 | 8 | 578 |

1

2

# Looking Westward

Late in the eighteenth century the Duc d'Orléans —who, as Louis Philippe, a generation later became king of France—visited America with his two younger brothers. On Washington's advice this trio made a tour of the western country, pausing on their way to enjoy a picnic at the Genesee Falls in New York (1), site of the future city of Rochester. The victories of the Revolution, Washington observed, had won America "a new Empire" in the West. The person who did more than any other to translate Washington's vision of empire into a reality in New York was William Cooper (2), who first explored the western part of the state in 1785 and who in 1789 settled in the infant village of Cooperstown on Lake Otsego. Thirty years later the New York artist S. F. B. Morse recorded the enduring charm of that lake and its environs (3). Later in his life Cooper boasted that he had settled more acres than any other man in America, and that there were "forty thousand souls holding directly or indirectly under me." In 1807 another French traveler sketched her impression of Utica (4), which an enthusiastic reporter about that time described as a "great emporium of European and other foreign goods with which the traders here supply a considerable portion of the country to the westward." A bit later, a transplanted Frenchman, Donatien Le Ray de Chaumont, built the handsome house (5) that still stands at Leraysville, New York.

# The War of 1812

In 1811 the United States was battling Britain on two fronts: at sea, where armed merchantmen and frigates fought each other for passage through the sea lanes; and in the West, where Indians, under British influence, confronted American armies. But war was not declared until June 1812. New York Harbor was blockaded. American armies passed through the port of Buffalo (1) to face the British in Canada. British expeditions attacked and captured Fort Niagara (2) and Fort Ontario at Oswego. In July 1814 thousands of British troops were poised in Montreal, ready to advance down the Hudson and take Albany, as Burgoyne had planned to do in 1777. To oppose them, some four thousand American troops under General Alexander Macomb were entrenched in the village of Plattsburgh on Lake Champlain. Each side heavily depended on naval support. On September 11, action began on lake and land. It is said that the British commander Sir George Prevost (3), viewing the naval engagement, predicted it would take just forty minutes to dispose of the American fleet under Commodore Thomas Macdonough (4). In the action that ensued (5), almost the entire British naval squadron was captured, and the British ground forces made a hurried retreat. The great offensive had ended. A contemporary poem rejoiced over the memorable victory (6).

4

5

## COMMODORE
## MACDONOUGH's VICTORY;

O FREEMEN, raise a joyous strain!
    Aloft the Eagle towers,
"*We've met the enemy*" again—
    Again have made them 'ours!'

Champlain! the cannon's thundering voice,
    Proclaims thy waters free;
Thy forest-waving hills rejoice,.
    And echo—*Victory* !.

The striped flag upon thy wave,.
    Triumphantly appears,
And to invested landsmen, brave,.
    A star of promise bears.

Now to the world Fame's trumpet sounds
    The deed with new applause,
While from a *Conquer'd Fleet* resounds,
    Our seamen's loud huzzas.

Britannia, round thy haggard brows
    Bind bitter wormwood still;
For lo ! again thy standard bows
    To valiant Yankee skill.

But; O ! what chaplet can be found
    M ACDONOUGH's brows to grace ?
'Tis done ! the glorious wreath is bound;
    Which time can ne'er efface,

And still a just—a rich reward,
    His country has to give;
He shall be first in her regard,
    And with her PERRY live !

Columbia ! though thy cannon's roar
    On inland seas prevail,
And thee alone—while round each shore
    Outnumbering ships assail.

Yet deed with deed, and name with name.
    Thy gallant sons shall blend,
Till the bright arch of naval fame,.
    O'er the broad ocean bend !.

6

# West Point

1

From trying and bitter experience in the field, George Washington was painfully aware of the inadequacies of the militia system in wartime crises. Supported by Alexander Hamilton and Henry Knox, he urged the establishment of a school to develop a base of military skill upon which the nation could depend in national emergencies. Finally, in 1802, such an academy was authorized by Act of Congress, to be situated on the escarpment at West Point, where there was still a Revolutionary War fort (1). A few graduates performed brilliantly in the War of 1812, but by 1817 affairs at the little academy had become a scandal. To correct matters, recently elected President James Monroe appointed as the new superintendent Brevet Major Sylvanus Thayer (2), a graduate of Dartmouth and in 1805 of West Point, and a serious student of military science. Smartly uniformed cadets (3) were introduced to the strict discipline that has ever since characterized the institution. Thayer's complete overhaul of the curriculum and the plan at the Point earned him the sobriquet "Father of the Military Academy." During his administration, the school, with its meticulously drilled cadets marching with utmost precision on the plain (4) overlooking the lordly Hudson, became one of the nation's showplaces.

2

3

4

## The Erie Canal

Two years after the War of 1812 was formally concluded, work commenced on the construction of the Erie Canal, the greatest engineering feat thus far attempted in the nation. The guiding genius of this colossal undertaking was DeWitt Clinton, canal commissioner and later governor of the state (1), who in 1817 persuaded the legislature to authorize the project. Even Thomas Jefferson with his vision of the future had observed that building such a waterway through 350 miles of wilderness was "little short of madness." New machinery in the form of great hoists to remove stumps and full-grown trees, and devices to cut deep-lying roots, were employed to clear the way for the giant cut through the wooded land; a new variety of cement was used to solidify the stonework (2). By 1825 Clinton's "Big Ditch" was completed, and by means of this artificial river New York's commercial empire was able to reach far into the western hinterland. Almost immediately, merchandise and produce of all description, travelers and migrants of every stripe, found their way to and fro along what was now the major thoroughfare of the country (3). The opening of the canal was probably the most important occasion in the history of New York Harbor. To celebrate the event, City Hall burst into a "Magnificent and Extraordinary" display of fireworks (4). When, as a symbolic ritual, a keg of water from Lake Erie was emptied into the Atlantic, a flotilla of twenty-two steamboats, among other vessels, was on hand to witness the proceeding (5). New York City's claim to be the "great commercial emporium" of America was now firmly clinched.

The busy trade that developed along the Erie Canal is depicted in an aquatint showing a canal lock in an unidentified canalside town around 1830.

## Erie Canal Cities

At almost every point the canal touched, it seemed, new towns sprang into being, old towns were charged with fresh vitality, all prepared to share in the passing commerce. According to one tourist guide, in 1821 Lockport boasted just two houses; with the completion of the canal a few years later, five ascending and five descending locks, "the most stupendous work on the whole route," made that site a key point on the canal, and Lockport flourished (1). Wheat grown in western parts of the state, formerly fed to pigs or converted into whisky on the spot because of the cost of transporting it elsewhere, could now be moved to seaboard markets for a few cents per bushel. As its population soared, Rochester quickly became the foremost flour-milling center of the country. Its great granite mills at the upper falls of the Genesee River (2) were called "the most stupendous works of modern art." The growth of Buffalo, the western terminal of the canal, was almost explosive. In 1810 the site had been a frontier outpost (3); several decades later, with its handsome stores, its fine churches, its hotels, its theaters, and its "harbour full of shipping and magnificent steam-boats" (4), the city reminded one astonished traveler of Aladdin's magic palace, sprung up virtually overnight on a lake shore. Albany (5) was the hub of the canal trade. It was a common occurrence for fifty gaily painted canal boats to leave there in a single day, laden with cargoes and passengers headed for the West.

1

3

4

As the nineteenth century advanced, New York City became far and away the nation's chief seaport, "a great open window to the world." New York was a city of ships, hemmed along its waterfront by a dense pattern of masts and bowsprits, as South Street was shown in a print issued in 1834 (1). About that same time another artist pictured the city's ample harbor teeming with craft of every description and from all parts of the world—a spectacle that brought crowds of landsmen to the waterfront to watch and wonder (2). In the autumn of 1817 a new era of maritime history had opened with the announcement that a fleet of transatlantic packet ships would operate out of New York on a fixed and regular schedule (3), regardless of wind and weather. These pioneering, square-rigged vessels of what was to be known as the Black Ball line—opposite is one of them, the *James Foster, Jr.* (4)—averaged twenty-three days on the eastward crossing to Liverpool and forty days on the return voyage against head winds. Within a few years they were carrying most of the passenger and freight trade of the Atlantic. As one consequence of the city's seafaring activities, New York became the major shipbuilding center in the United States. The Smith and Dimon yards (5), although not by any means the largest of such operations, turned out some important ships, including the first extreme clipper built in this country. In 1833 New York shipyards were responsible for constructing twenty-six ships and barks, seven brigs, thirty-six schooners, and five steamboats.

5

# Steamboats on the Hudson

The first commercially successful steamboat in the United States was Robert Fulton's *North River Steamboat of Clermont,* popularly known in later years simply as the *Clermont.* In 1802 Fulton (1)—an inventor, engineer, and artist—contracted to construct such a vessel for Robert R. Livingston (2), who held a monopoly on steamboating in New York waters. (Among his many other distinctions, Livingston had as chancellor of the state of New York administered the oath at Washington's inauguration.) History was made in 1807 when the *Clermont,* sounding "like the devil in a sawmill," chugged its way from New York to Albany in thirty-two hours. In 1810 a print was issued in France, after a drawing by an eyewitness, showing the craft, probably rebuilt and enlarged, passing West Point on one of its trips up the river (3). A view of Fulton's third Hudson River boat, the *Paragon* (4), was painted by a visiting Russian artist, to whom the vessel was a spectacle of wonder with its spacious and elegant accommodations, where one could enjoy "the best wines, all manner of dainties, and even ice-cream in the hot season." The *Paragon* was, he exclaimed, "a whole floating town!" Steamboating quickly caught the popular imagination, and the number of such vessels plying the Hudson rapidly multiplied. Travelers swarmed to steamboat landings (5) in response to broadsides issued by companies competing for business (6). Meanwhile, in 1811 Fulton and Livingston introduced steamferry service between Manhattan Island and the New Jersey shore; by the 1830s their ferries handled most of the traffic across the lower Hudson (7).

## 6

# HUDSON RIVER
## Steam-Boat Line.

### Constitution,
Captain W. J. WISWALL.

### Constellation,
Captain R. G. CRUTTENDEN.

## DAILY.

THESE new and splendid Boats will be despatched, DAILY, from New-York and Albany, during the summer months; commencing their regular trips, under this arrangement, on Monday the 5th June. Leaving the wharf, foot of Cortlandt-street, New-York, at 10 o'clock A. M. and the wharf near the Steam-Boat Office, South Market-street, Albany, at 9 o'clock.

When practicable the Boats will come to at the wharves of Newburgh, Poughkeepsie, Catskill and Hudson. At Rhinebeck and Kingston a convenient barge will constantly be in readiness to receive and land passengers. At the other intermediate places, passengers will be received and landed whenever it can be effected with safety.

These Boats are of the first class, and for extensive and airy accommodations, speed, and quiet motion of their engines, and skilful management, are not surpassed by any boat navigating the Hudson River; and the proprietors assure the public that the most assiduous attention will be paid to the safety and comfort of Passengers.—Agents for this Line,

A. N. HOFFMAN, *No.* 71 *Dey-street, New-York.*
T. BARTHOLOMEW, *South Market-street, Albany.*

☞ All freight and baggage at the risk of the owners. Freight of light articles one shilling per cubic foot.

*MAY 23, 1826.*          Child & Wells, Printers, corner Greenwich & Vesey st.

# The Hudson

The Hudson is by no means the largest nor the longest of rivers, but it is without question one of the most picturesque. From its tiny beginnings in the Adirondacks until its majestic entry into the Atlantic, it is only about 315 miles long. Along its course the Hudson has cut its way through ancient rocks and mountainous terrain, fashioning a landscape of irresistible allure to artists. During the last century particularly, artists celebrated the beauty of the Hudson River Valley. The popularity of the view from West Point (1) was enhanced by colorful historical associations dating from the Revolution. From Mount Ida, at the Falls of Cohoes, just north of Troy, one could observe the junction of the Hudson and the Mohawk (2). The appropriately named villa, Undercliff (3), near Cold Spring, was the riverside seat of General George P. Morris. Near Hudson (4), riverside roads provided a stirring view of the Catskill Mountains. Many artists depicted the commanding escarpment on which West Point was built; Robert Havell's painting (5) shows West Point and an encampment of tents on the plain below.

Pages 102 and 103: In the early days of steam navigation, Peekskill was an important landing place.

3

4
5

# The Hudson River School

Reporting on his visit to the United States in the 1830s, the English naval commander and author Captain Frederick Marryat observed that the Hudson River was "incomparably more beautiful" than the Rhine; it was as he imagined the Rhine to have been in Caesar's day. The first artist to capture that semiwild beauty with his brush was Thomas Cole (1), a virtually self-taught English immigrant who settled in New York in 1825. In the years thereafter Cole spent weeks and months walking and sketching his way through the Catskill Mountains that overlook the Hudson. His work immediately attracted attention, and he was already prospering when he painted "The Clove, Catskills" in 1827 (2). Cole strongly advised young painters of the necessity of outdoor, on-the-spot drawing of nature, as he himself did in such sketches as the "Highlands of the Hudson Near New Windsor" (3). His work strongly influenced a group of painters known as the Hudson River school, an unorganized fraternity of able artists, whose meticulous portraits of the hills, lakes, valleys, and rivers of the state preserve a rich and lyrical record of the primitive landscape. Asher B. Durand (4), Cole's fellow artist and frequent sketching companion, was a pioneer in painting out of doors. English-born Robert Havell, Jr., came to America and settled in New York State, where he recorded aspects of the surrounding countryside. In an unidentified view, he included the figures of two artists at work in the open (5). In 1869 John Frederick Kensett, one of the most prominent landscapists of the day, painted his impression of Lake George, nestled in the wilderness of the Adirondack foothills (6).

3  4

5

6

# Mount's Long Island

The commonplace aspects of rural life on Long Island in the middle years of the last century, its accustomed routines and bucolic pleasures, were depicted with engaging candor and a skilled brush by the local painter William Sidney Mount, who was born into a farming family in Setauket in 1807. His canvases are self-explanatory, as they were intended to be, and reflect the artist's intimate understanding of the daily activity he recorded. The titles he gave his paintings are suggestive but hardly necessary: "Farmers Nooning" (1), "Cider Making" (2), "Long Island Farmhouses" (3), "Eel Spearing at Setauket" (4), "The Power of Music" (5), and so on. A number of his works were reproduced in Europe, where they were widely circulated. Mount was the first American painter to treat black subjects with dignity and individuality.

4

5

# Literary New York

4

While the artists of the Hudson River school were celebrating and documenting the natural wonders of the state with their paintings and drawings, a number of talented novelists and poets were creating new visions of New York with their writings. The historical whimsies of Washington Irving (1) and the frontier romances of James Fenimore Cooper (2), both culled from the lore of the land, provided the state with a legendary past that is unforgettable. Whatever their origin, today's New Yorkers are all the spiritual heirs of the bearded Rip Van Winkle (3), and of Leatherstocking (4) and the other characters who animated the fictions of the two authors. As Irving wove its magic into his stories, the Hudson River became one of the world's enchanted waterways, and his stories were widely read on both sides of the Atlantic. Out of his love for the forested land to the north and west of the Hudson, Cooper spun tales that have been called America's own "Arabian Nights of the Frontier" and that were read in translation throughout the western world. (Franz Schubert pleaded from his deathbed for still another Cooper novel to distract him from his mortal illness.) In 1825 William Cullen Bryant (5) fled New England for New York with his reputation as a poet already made in America and soon to spread to Europe. His lyrical nature poetry was an inspiration to Thomas Cole, with whom Bryant hiked in the Catskills. As a memorial to their friendship, the two kindred spirits were painted by Asher B. Durand as they stood at one of their favorite mountain haunts (6).

1

2

3

4

5

Although New York City was moving uptown at a formidable rate, in the 1820s Broadway, neighboring Bowling Green, was still New York's stylish residential quarter and a fashionable mall which, wrote James Fenimore Cooper in 1828, vied with any promenade in the world (1). The house at the extreme left in the illustration was occupied by George Washington during the early days of the Revolution. At the time, Greek Revival styles in architecture, furniture, and decoration enjoyed a great vogue. An ideal interior in that fashion was designed by the prominent contemporary architect Alexander J. Davis for John C. Stevens of New York (2). Another stylish interior of the period, depicting a reception in 1840 at the Broadway home of Dr. John C. Cheesman, was rendered in a silhouette by Augustin Edouart (3). Behind its elegant Greek Revival facade, the Astor House, built on Broadway in the 1830s as New York's most sumptuous hotel (4), featured such extraordinary and novel conveniences as baths and toilets on every floor, supplied with water raised by a steam pump. In 1838 Davis undertook to create a summer retreat near Tarrytown, New York, for William Paulding and his son, Philip. This time the architect designed a structure in the Gothic Revival manner (5), of such an elaborate appearance that Philip Hone predicted it would become known as "Paulding's Folly." Enlarged by subsequent owners and named Lyndhurst, the building still stands, one of the prized possessions of the National Trust for Historic Preservation. Some of the original furnishings made for Paulding in the Gothic style are still preserved in the house (6).

6

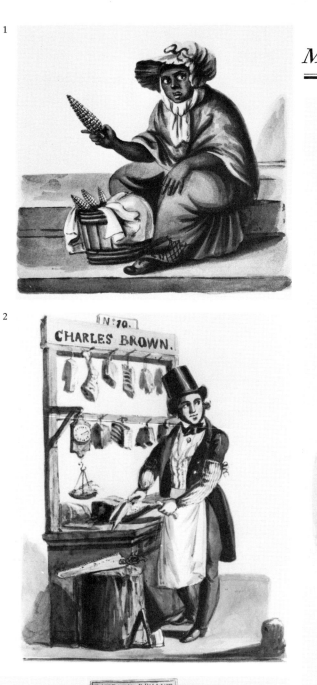

In the middle of the nineteenth century, household products and provisions of almost every sort were hawked about the crowded streets of New York City by a picturesque assortment of vendors, whose cries advertising their wares were pitched above the other noises of the metropolis. About 1840 the Italian artist Nicolino V. Calyo, a perceptive and sympathetic observer, made a series of watercolor sketches of these colorful and sometimes well-known hucksters. Young bloods of the Five Points district fought for the favors of the wittiest and prettiest of the Hot Corn girls (1). Charles Brown the butcher (2) sold twelve pounds of mutton for $1.50, for which he was accused of overcharging. Root beer, however, sold for three cents a glass (3), and Patrick Bryant sold liberally salted oysters for a penny or two apiece (4). Charcoal could be had from the self-professed "biggest rogue in the world" (5), and cheap ice brought to the city from the winter's harvest at upstate Rockland Lake (6) had by now become "an article of necessity." Strawberries were offered that were "Fine, ripe and red!" (7).

7

# Tenements and Shanties

Not far uptown from the fashionable residential section, the city's Five Points, a name applied to a district of slums, became a spawning ground for crime, vice, and misery. The unidentified artist who depicted a street scene of the neighborhood about 1829 portrays himself in the center foreground holding a handkerchief to his nostrils to allay the stench (1). Here gathered the worst of such New York gangs as the Soap Locks (2), the Plug Uglies, the Dead Rabbits, and others who broke the peace and one another's skulls, often in murderous earnest, beyond the control of the primitive police system of the time. Here, too, in miserable tenements (3), lived the poorest New Yorkers. In the year 1860 Mr. Peter Williams ran a basement "ballroom" on Baxter Street where jig dancing was a popular form of entertainment (4). Farther uptown, on and around the present site of the United Nations, a village of rickety and filthy shanties (5) housed immigrant laborers hired to level hills and valleys and to grade avenues and streets in preparation for the advancing urban frontier. As the accompanying illustrations reveal, omnipresent roaming pigs helped dispose of the garbage that littered the streets. In its issue for August 13, 1859, *Frank Leslie's Illustrated Newspaper* pictured a police roundup in which pigs were driven to the city's pound (6).

2

114

3

# Urban Traffic

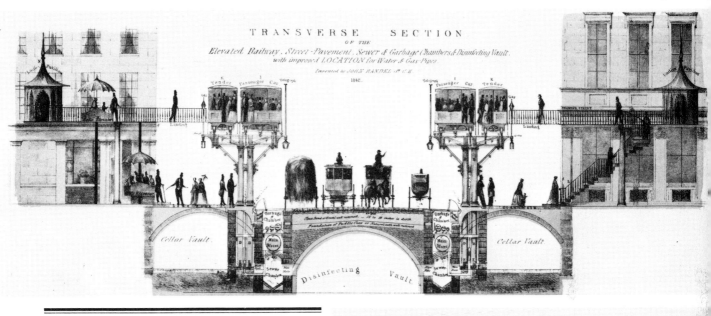

By the 1830s street traffic had emerged as one of New York's most persistent and growing problems, a problem made more vexing by the proliferation of omnibuses that crowded the main thoroughfares. An illustration opposite (1) shows them passing to and fro along Broadway before Saint Paul's Chapel about 1831. The limits of the city had already expanded to make the distance from home to place of business or main shopping center beyond convenient walking range, and such conveyances had become necessary. In 1848 an English visitor remarked that all Broadway seemed to be paved with them. As early as 1825 an elevated railway had been proposed to alleviate congestion, and in 1848 elaborate plans for such a construction were drawn up (2, 3). Stationary steam engines would propel passenger cars along endless ropes; gas lights would brighten the way; and "safe elevators" would lift ladies to restful pavilions where they could meet their friends. However, another twenty years passed before the first "El" was actually constructed—along somewhat different lines. Meanwhile, traffic worsened. At midcentury one visitor from abroad observed that when crossing Broadway, a perilous adventure pictured in a contemporary magazine illustration (4), her great concern was to reach the other side alive.

# Water for the City

One of the greatest engineering achievements of the mid-nineteenth century, the Croton Aqueduct, was completed in 1842 after five years of planning and building. This remarkable system tapped the Croton River, some forty miles from New York City, and carried its waters over hills and valleys to provide the metropolis for the first time with an adequate water supply. High Bridge (1), which carried the water across the Harlem River, has been compared with the finest aqueducts of ancient Rome in grace and strength. Extravagant demonstrations were held to celebrate the great event (2), and New Yorkers traveled uptown to view the distributing reservoir, designed in the Egyptian style (3) and built on the site of the present New York Public Library. "Nothing is talked of or thought of in New York but Croton Water," Philip Hone wrote in his diary. As water poured from city faucets, plumbers were in a position to develop kitchen and indoor bathroom facilities in unprecedented ways (4), although it was some years before the new conveniences became standard equipment for the average home. Firemen, still enthusiastic volunteers rather than professionals, fought for the honor of being first at the hydrants that were now in use replacing the old hand pumps (5).

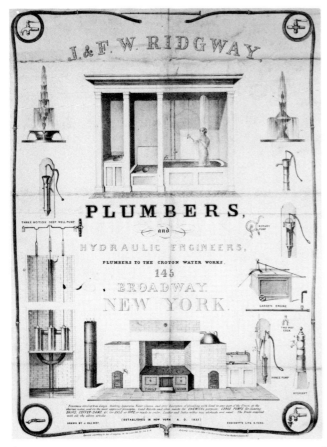

# Gaslight

The main streets of New York City and other communities in the state which could warrant the expense were traditionally lighted by whale-oil lamps set upon posts and tended by an appointed lamplighter (1). Such illumination, it had been complained, barely made the darkness visible. In 1824 the New York *Evening Post* reported that gas was a far superior illuminant for homes and public buildings as well as for streets. A year later there were already seventeen thousand gas burners in use, and by 1830 there were gas lampposts on a number of the city's streets. About 1837 the visiting English artist George Harvey painted "Night-Fall: St. Thomas' Church, Broadway, New York," showing the new lighting in operation; a detail of the painting shows the gas lamp lighter going about his business (2). Edgar Allan Poe complained in 1840 that gaslight was "totally inadmissible within doors . . . and positively offensive" in general. But in its glow, the belles at a ball at New York's Metropolitan Hotel in 1859 still managed to display their charms (3). In 1844 a massive and elaborate gas chandelier was installed in the Van Rensselaer Manor House at Albany (4). An architect's drawing of a lamppost proposed for New York's Central Park (5) is a model of simple elegance.

1

2

**WHOLESALE STORE**
**AT**
**LYON'S FALLS!**
**THE RAILROAD TERMINUS!**

A. H. TYLER & Co. would respectfully announce to the Merchants and Citizens of LEWIS and adjoining Counties, that they have on hand and are daily receiving A LARGE STOCK of

**GROCERIES!**
**DRY GOODS!**
**BOOTS and SHOES, Nails, &c.**

Which they will sell at a small Advance of Cost.

**Call & Examine our Teas!**

Look at our
**SUGARS, COFFEES, PRINTS and**
**Ready Made Clothing!**

3

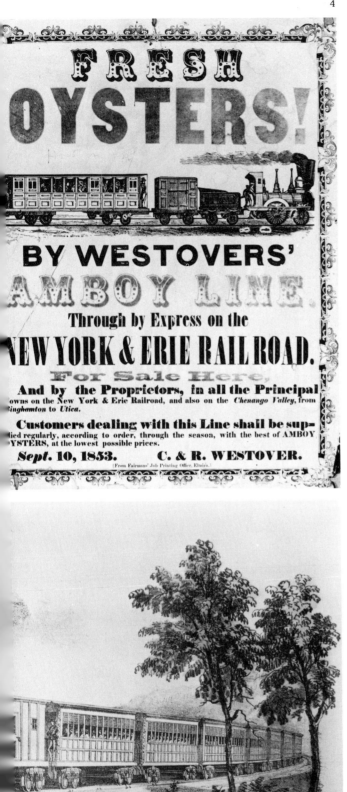

New York's first railroad—the famous Mohawk and Hudson, which ran between Albany and Schenectady—was opened on August 9, 1831. In the presence of thousands of spectators, the tiny steam-powered *De Witt Clinton* successfully pulled three passenger cars adapted from stagecoaches (1), reaching the unheard-of speed of sixteen miles an hour. Almost immediately thereafter a series of additional short lines were projected across the state, most of them planned to attract trade from the surrounding countryside into individual towns, as the line at Lyon's Falls, north of Utica, did (2), rather than to connect separate regions of the state. However, such lines were gradually consolidated into larger systems. The popular printmakers Currier and Ives issued a lithograph showing an 1842 scene on the railroad connecting Boston and Albany (3). In that year, representatives of various lines agreed to arrange the passage of through trains all the way from Albany to Buffalo. By 1853 refrigerator car service made it possible for towns in central New York and the Southern Tier to enjoy rare delicacies such as oysters, shipped from the coast by the New York and Erie Railroad (4). After the first carload of refrigerated butter was shipped to Boston one hot June, the value of dairy farms in the Ogdensburg–Rouses Point area increased 100 percent with the new promise of year-round markets. The Erie was planned to connect the Hudson River and Lake Erie by way of the Southern Tier. When it was finished in 1851 it was the longest continuous railroad line in the world. After ten years of planning and construction under the direction of John A. Roebling, the first large railroad suspension bridge in the world was built over the Niagara River to span the gorge separating Canada and the United States (5). That engineering triumph was almost as great a spectacle as Niagara Falls.

# The Steamboats' Heyday

Less than a generation after Fulton's pioneering voyage, the Hudson had become a broad thoroughfare teeming with the traffic of its steamboats. At midcentury nearly a million people patronized the river steamers in any one year, as many as a thousand in a single passage. Developments in size and speed were remarkable. A Currier & Ives print of the S. S. *St. John* suggests the slim and sleek elegance of these side-wheelers (1). The press referred to "our mile-long steamers"— the largest to be built before the Civil War was 371 feet long—and to the "fastest boats in the world"; in 1843 one sped from Albany to New York in just seven hours and twenty-one minutes. Races such as that between the *Isaac Newton* and the *Francis Skiddy* were sporting events (2), with the fastest boat attracting the most business, unless it blew up and burnt down in the contest, as did the *Henry Clay* in 1852 (3) with an appalling loss of life. These were, as the press claimed, "the grandest palace drawing-room steamers in the world," a boast justified by the rococo extravagance of the saloon of the S. S. *Drew* (4). Within a few years of Fulton's first run, steamboats had also ventured into the more open waters of Long Island Sound and the Great Lakes. About 1840 the English artist George Harvey painted this scene at Portland Pier on Lake Erie as passengers rushed to board a departing steamer (5).

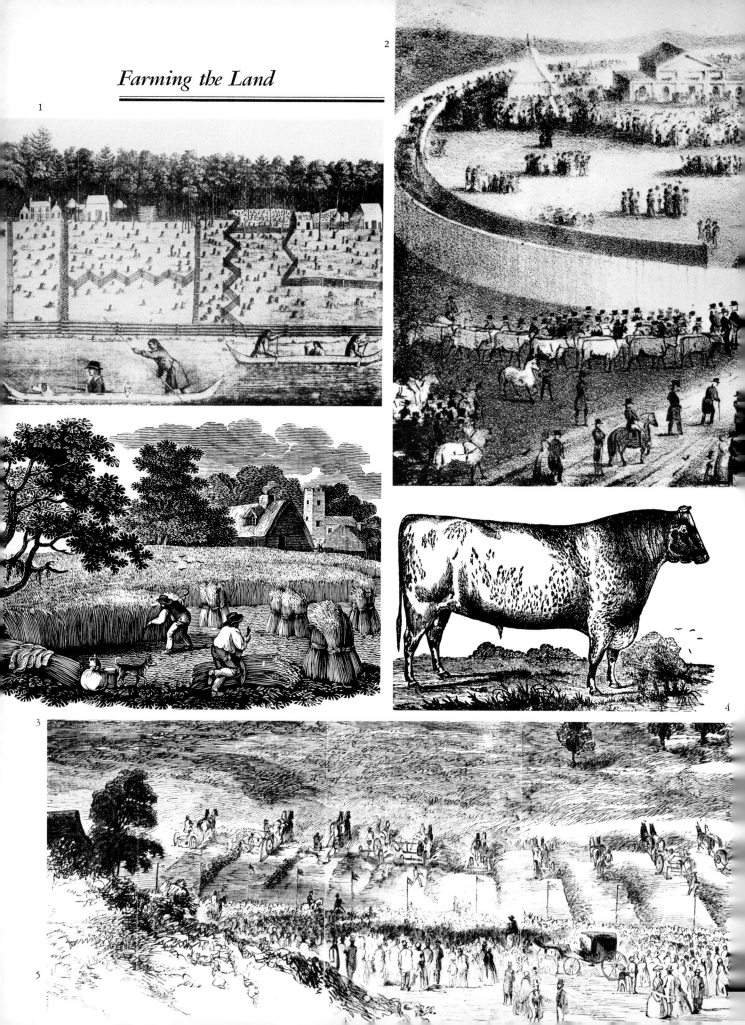

# Farming the Land

Early in the nineteenth century, Washington Irving described the fields of western New York where the occasional pioneer farmer worked about his rude cabin amid the charred stumps of yesterday's forests (1). Reports that the land thus cleared could yield prodigious crops sent the hopeful to that area in huge numbers to try their luck. The amount of improved farmland in the state increased from about 1 million acres in 1784 to 5 million acres in 1821. Within a generation, the Genesee Valley was transformed from an unrelieved wilderness into "the granary of the nation," centering around the Rochester mills which, it seemed, produced more flour than the world could need. Throughout New York, as in other regions, county and state fairs, such as the 1846 Auburn Fair (2), were held to demonstrate publicly the abundance of the soil and the industry of the region's farmers (3). Prize cattle, such as the Durham bull named Archer, owned by Colonel J. M. Sherwood of Auburn, New York (4), were exhibited, and their somewhat glorified likenesses were reproduced in farm journals to promote the good care and feeding of livestock. Farmers vied with each other demonstrating their skills; at left is a competition among reapers and mowers, which took place at a Syracuse Fair in 1857 (5). Outstanding apples, such as the "King of Tompkins County," were celebrated in popular prints (6).

6

127

# Rent Riots

In the 1830s substantial areas in New York were still owned by descendants of the Dutch patroons and English manor lords, a landed aristocracy whose tenant farmers leased their small holdings on semifeudal terms. The tight-knit privileged families held almost 2 million acres on which more than a quarter of a million persons lived. When Stephen Van Rensselaer (1) died in 1839, his holdings alone included some 700,000 acres centering about Albany. Such long-established arrangements were an anachronism in America. As early as the 1760s there had been popular uprisings against that archaic system, but they were suppressed. Now, in the 1830s and 1840s, antirent protests took on the nature of guerrilla warfare. At the warning sound of a tin dinner horn, militant units of farmers ludicrously disguised as Indians wearing calico gowns ("calico Indians," as they were called) would rally to challenge agents commissioned to collect overdue rents or to foreclose on tenants' properties (2). In 1839 Governor William Seward felt obliged to call out the state militia to support a sheriff who had been dispatched as a rent collector (3). The countryside was aflame with grassroots protests against "patroonry." Mass meetings were held (4), and there was violence and bloodshed. In the end the tenants won their struggle largely through court action and political pressure.

## ATTENTION!
## ANTI-RENTERS'
### AWAKE! AROUSE!

**A Meeting of the friends of Equal Rights** will be held on

in the Town of                                    at        O'clock.

Let the opponents of Patroonry rally in their strength. A great crisis is approaching. Now is the time to strike. The minions of Patroonry are at work. No time is to be lost. Awake! Arouse! and

Strike 'till the last armed foe expires.
Strike for your altars and your fires—
Strike for the green graves of your sires.
God and your happy homes!

☞ **The Meeting will be addressed by PETER FINKLE and other Speakers.**

Broadside in New York State Library, Albany

1

2

3

During the middle decades of the last century, New York became the indisputable center of American journalism, with an influence that radiated throughout the country. For almost half a century after 1829 William Cullen Bryant, editor of the *Evening Post,* fearlessly attacked every threat to free speech and supported unpopular causes he considered worthy. In 1833 Benjamin Day published the first issue of *The Sun* (1), a penny journal that mixed sensationalism with daily reporting of topical developments. Soon afterward, the Scottish immigrant James Gordon Bennett followed suit with his New York *Herald.* Technological improvements in printing made it possible to print thousands of papers per hour in the *Herald*'s press room (2). Horace Greeley (3), who founded the New York *Tribune* in 1841, was probably the most influential newspaper editor of his time, a man who was sensitive to moral issues and who militantly crusaded for reforms that ranged from abolition and temperance to feminism and vegetarianism. One of the most enduring of these great dailies, the New York *Times,* founded in 1851, was soon housed in a structure that towered "upwards of eighty feet above the pavement" (4). The Albany *Argus* (5) was one of the leading Democratic journals in the country. Across the state the Buffalo *Republican* (6) spoke for the opposing political faction.

# Correspondents

The New York *Herald* boasted of its fleet of speedy clipper ships that brought news from overseas in record time, picturing them in 1846 (1), along with a spoofing allusion to the firm's "Chinese war correspondent" (2). Distribution of the published news was in good part delegated to such children as Thomas Le Clear painted in 1853 in his "Buffalo Newsboy" (3). Visiting foreigners were struck by the wild energy of those small city lads who, as one Englishman observed, rushed "hither and thither with their arms full of wisdom, at a penny an installment" (4). Another Englishman observed that America was becoming "the land of the general reader," who had a strong addiction to his newspaper (5). By the middle of the century New York journalism had already become a highly competitive field, in which advanced technology, shrewd merchandising, advertising, and entertaining features all played their parts, along with prompt and responsible reporting of the latest news. A painting by William Sidney Mount (6) suggests the eagerness with which the artist's Long Island neighbors scanned the *Tribune* for the most recent reports from the California gold mines in 1850.

*133*

1  2

3

134

4

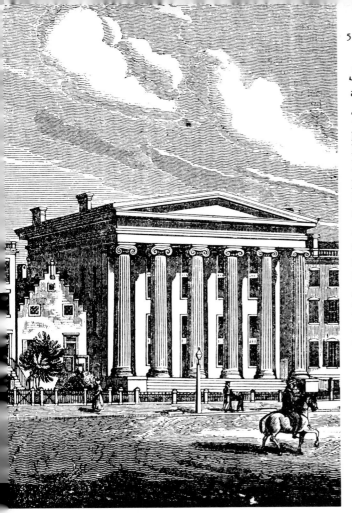

## Schools for the Young

The first free school in New York City supported partly by municipal funds was opened in 1809. Public School Number 1, at Tryon Row and Park Row (1), can be seen in the background of a portrait of George T. Trimble, president of the Public Schools Society. For some time to come, school accommodations were not always adequate. A schoolteacher of the 1840s was pictured in a contemporary drawing instructing a class with the aid of a phonetic chart in what appears to be a basement room (2). The worse plight of those children who could not or would not attend such halls of learning was suggested by a poignant engraving issued at midcentury (3). The "Institution of Messrs. Abbott, for the Education of Young Ladies, at 412 Houston St.," as shown in the school's catalogue for 1846, offered selected studies considered appropriate for members of the opposite sex (4). Increasing attention was given to the education of girls. The *American Magazine* in 1835 applauded Albany's new Female Academy with an expression of hope that improving girls' education would provide for "the elevation of the female character and the increase of female influence in society" (5). In rural districts the one-room schoolhouse continued to dispense education to both sexes at the elementary level with very indifferent results (6).

1

2  3

4

## Higher Education

5

As the nineteenth century advanced, colleges pro-liferated throughout the state, most of them en-joying generous subsidies from the state govern-ment. King's College had been reincorporated as Columbia College in 1787 under acts providing for a University of the State of New York. At Schenectady, Union College, chartered in 1795, developed into and long remained the largest in-stitution of higher learning in the country. A ground plan for the college, with its buildings surrounding a broad mall dominated by a classical rotunda flanked by formal gardens (1), was drawn up in 1813 by Joseph Jacques Ramée, an émigré architect from France. The U-shaped main quad-rangle, with dormitories at the two ends (2), rep-resents part of that unique plan. For sixty-two years Eliphalet Nott, inventor of the first anthra-cite coal base-burner stove, served as the college's president. Unlike most of the other early colleges, Union was nonsectarian. Hamilton College at Clin-ton, New York, was founded in 1812 by Congre-gationalists as a training school for missionaries (3). Seven years later, Colgate was established by Baptists with similar aims (4). In 1831 the Uni-versity of the City of New York (now New York University) was chartered, and classes began the following year. A plan for the building designed in the Greek Revival style by the well-known archi-tectural firm of Town and Davis (5) was dis-carded for one in the Gothic Revival manner by the same architects (6). It was in this structure on the east side of Washington Square that Sam-uel F. B. Morse, professor of art, carried on his experiments in electrical telegraphy and that Sam-uel Colt perfected his "peacemaker." The building was demolished in 1894.

6

137

## Entertainment

New York's Park Theater, which had opened in 1798 with a performance of Shakespeare's *As You Like It,* was destroyed by fire in 1820. Construction was immediately begun on its replacement, a building which was designed to seat 2,500 persons. A watercolor painted by John Searle in 1822 shows the actors Charles Mathews and Miss Johnson performing at the new theater in a scene from Moncrieff's *Monsieur Touson* before an audience that included many distinguished New Yorkers (1). The following year, William Dunlap, a playwright-artist, painted a scene from the dramatization of James Fenimore's Cooper's historical novel *The Spy* (2). New York's rank and file found more varied entertainment by taking a boat trip across the Hudson to Hoboken's "Elysian Fields," where, among other diversions, they could row in brightly painted boats, stroll through the wooded park, or enjoy an exciting ride on the "pleasure railway" (3). In 1835, when Fanny Kemble visited the site, she was impressed by the "well-being and contentment" of the working classes and tradespeople she observed there. For those with other interests the Union Course on Long Island staged highly popular horse races. The great regional race between the northern horse American Eclipse (4) and the Virginia-foaled Sir Henry (5), held in 1823, attracted a crowd of about 100,000 spectators, some of whom came from distant states to witness the event. More than $200,000 was wagered on the outcome. (Eclipse won.) When the renowned horses Peytona and Fashion met at the same course twenty-two years later for a $20,000 purse (6), traffic en route to the race was so heavy many almost missed the race.

1    2

3

4

5

6

**KNICKERBOCKER BALL CLUB.**

| FINES. | NAMES. | HANDS OUT. | RUNS. | REMARKS. |
|---|---|---|---|---|
| 1 | Turney | 1  3  2 | *1 | |
| 2 | Kubold | 1  3 | 1111 | |
| 3 | O'Brien | | 1111 | 6 *for swearing* |
| 4 | Dummond | 2  3 | 1141 | |
| 5 | Hunt | *1  1 | 111 | |
| 6 | Bogut | 2  2 | 1111 | |
| 7 | Ahtriey | 2  1 | 111 | |
| 8 | Tuhigraie | *1  2 | 11 | |
| 9 | Bivman | 2 | 1 | |
| | De Mott | 1  1 | | |

NEW-YORK,          184 .                                              UMPIRE.

The round of pleasures available to New Yorkers at midcentury was endlessly varied. In 1845 the Knickerbocker Base Ball Club of New York was organized by a bank clerk, Alexander Cartwright, and played its first match game on October 6. One of the contestants was "fined 6 cts. for swearing." It was the first recorded game of modern baseball, the forerunner of a championship game played in Brooklyn in 1860 (1), and won by the Excelsiors over the Atlantics, 23—4. One rare relic of the early days of baseball is the "game book" or box score surviving from the Knickerbocker's first game (2). Spectator sports included watching girls in fetching costumes bathing at Coney Island (3). When the Bostonian Thomas Wentworth Higginson, an apostle of "manly outdoor exercise," pronounced the benefits to be derived from ice skating, he excited renewed interest in that sport. In 1860 Winslow Homer painted a winter scene at New York's Central Park (4), where as many as fifty thousand skaters tried their runners on the frozen ponds of a winter's day. Offshore, the races of the New York Yacht Club, organized in 1844, attracted devotees of that sport (5), especially after the *America*, owned by five members of the club, defeated all comers in the race held at Cowes, England, in 1851 to determine the world's fastest sailing yacht. The Gem Saloon, an adjunct of the Broadway Theater, and boasting the largest mirror in New York (6), was a favorite haunt of city celebrities who enjoyed the indoor sport of tippling.

5

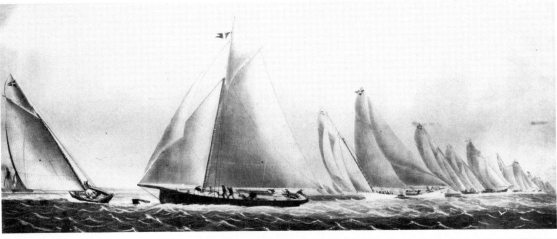

6

## Away for Vacation

The proliferation of railroads and steamboats made it easier for Americans to quit their cities for fresh-air holidays in relatively distant places. By 1833 there were two daily trains leaving Albany for Schenectady to connect with cars going to the fashionable watering place at Saratoga (1). "All the world is here," observed the diarist Philip Hone when he visited the popular spa in 1839. Entrepreneurs in resort towns throughout the state were building luxurious hotels to accommodate the swelling volume of vacationers. In 1823 construction was started on Catskill Mountain House (2), high in the Catskill Mountains but within less than a day's journey of New York City; it was to become one of the most phenomenal of early resort hotels. As the original structure expanded (3), it became a favorite retreat for such illustrious figures as William Cullen Bryant, James Fenimore Cooper, Washington Irving, Thomas Cole, and Jenny Lind —and in later years Oscar Wilde, Henry James, and a host of others. The famous structure was demolished in 1963. Historic Lake George in the foothills of the Adirondacks has been termed one of the most beautiful mountain lakes in the world. One of the early resort hotels that sprang up about the lake (4), with access by steamboat, was built near the site of Fort William Henry, which had been built in 1756 by Sir William Johnson to protect the portage between the lake and the Hudson.

2

3

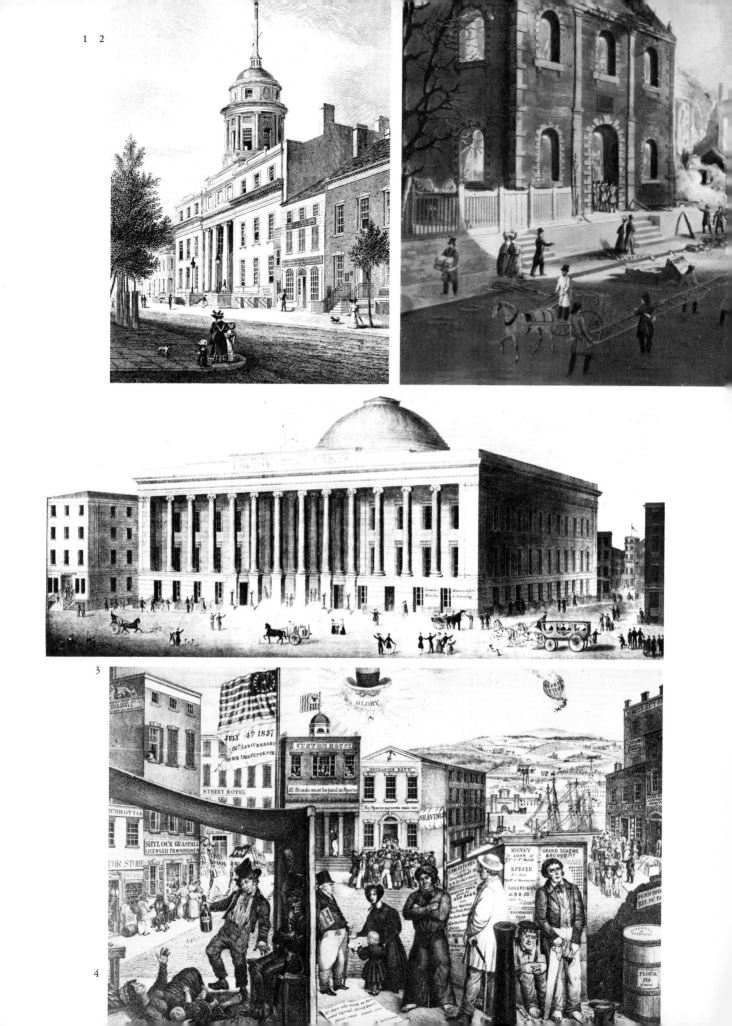

By the mid-1820s New York had replaced Philadelphia as the nation's principal center of business and finance. In 1823 the New York Merchant Exchange Company was incorporated with a capital of one million dollars, and shortly thereafter the organization built a marble "palace" to house its operations (1). On December 16, 1835, a disastrous fire consumed nearly seven hundred structures in the very heart of the city, including the Exchange (2). However, work was immediately started on an even more elaborate structure to replace the ruins (3). That vigorous spirit, remarked one visiting witness, proved that the city's commercial credit could withstand almost any shock. Ironically, in 1837, before those words could be put into print, America suffered the most serious yet of its periodic panics and depressions, a disaster satirized in a popular print of the time (4). By 1842, however, New York had completed a massive new custom house on Wall Street to accommodate the reborn and rapidly increasing business of the city, business that was avidly discussed by merchants, traders, and others on the street level (5). Within a relatively few years the Custom House (still standing as the United States Sub-Treasury) was considered "too contracted" for its purposes. On October 13, 1857, another panic spread throughout the country, bringing bankers and other concerned citizens out onto Wall Street to lament the latest bad news (6).

*Newcomers to the State*

5

Among the many different factors that inspired Europeans to emigrate to America, the lure of high wages played a large role. As a woodcut of about 1855 suggests, John Bull was unable to restrain Britons from responding to America's welcome (1). Between 1840 and 1900 more than two million Englishmen, Scots, and Welshmen went off to the New World, with New York the major port of debarkation. A contemporary painting shows the arrival of a crowded immigrant ship (2). At the left of the picture, at the tip of Manhattan Island, stands Castle Garden, which was made a reception center for immigrants in 1855. The junk *Keying,* probably the first Chinese vessel to visit America, is shown anchored offshore. The number of immigrants mounted dramatically from decade to decade. For the year ending September 30, 1820, the number was less than four thousand; in 1832 the figure rose to about thirty thousand; and in 1854 almost a third of a million aliens arrived at the port. Whole villages in Germany emigrated. Soon New York contained more Germans than any city in the world except Berlin and Vienna. In 1847 a series of cartoons in one German-American newspaper featured humorous episodes in the adventures of newcomers from the fatherland (3). Occasionally there were disgraceful exhibitions of intolerance by hoodlums who broke up German gatherings as "un-American" demonstrations (4). Among the most distinguished of all early immigrants from Germany was Carl Schurz, who became a major general in the Union Army and, later in his life, a distinguished and influential New York editor and author (5).

# *The Coming of the Green*

1

CONCERT
DUBLIN CELEBRATED
SHAMROCK LINE
AMERICAN PACKET
SHAMR
SISTER SHIP TO
FARES OUT
NEW YOR
CLASS

2

3

TO
EMIGRANTS
RETURNING
NEW YORK
TO
DUBLIN
BARQUE
WASHINGTON

4

The Irish, attracted by announcements that were posted throughout their land (1), arrived at New York in even greater numbers than the Germans. Thanks in good part to a potato famine in Ireland, more than 160,000 arrived in the single year of 1851. Like the tide of German immigration, this enormous influx of alien and poor Irishmen provoked some resentment among "real Americans" —that is, among those whose families had come to this country earlier, a spirit noted in a drawing that shows a young bootblack bowing in mock deference to a newly arrived Irish family (2). Successful immigrants who returned to Ireland to enjoy their prosperity among scenes of their leaner days were walking advertisements of the advantages to be found in the New World (3). In 1858 construction was started on St. Patrick's Cathedral (4), one of the largest and costliest structures in the city. In 1875, at a ceremony in the cathedral, John McCloskey was made the first American cardinal (5). Further evidence of the growing strength of the Irish in New York is a view of the St. Patrick's Day parade in 1874 (6), with a bust of the Irish patriot Daniel O'Connell in the foreground. The Irish have celebrated that religious, political, and folk festival in New York for more than two centuries.

## Religion and Reform

5

6

During the decades preceding the Civil War, New York provided fertile ground for a variety of groups and movements bent on finding special ways to salvation, of achieving the final redemption of man, or at least of improving man's earthly lot. The famous book of golden pages that is called the Book of Mormon was left on a New York hill for Joseph Smith to find in 1827 and to translate with the aid of diamond-lensed spectacles that lay conveniently beside it (1). On another New York hill, in 1844, William Miller, "a man mighty in the Scriptures" (2), gathered his white-robed followers to await the end of the world as they had known it and to hail the Second Coming of Christ, when they would be carried up to heaven. By meticulous calculation Miller had determined that this would come about on October 22 of that year, a prognostication ridiculed by skeptics, as a contemporary cartoon demonstrates (3). A few years later the first convention in history to argue the question of women's rights was held in Seneca Falls (4). In the late forties two sisters of Hydesville, New York, Maggie and Katie Fox (5), convinced a numerous following, including Horace Greeley, that the mysterious spirit rappings that could be heard wherever they appeared were true indications from the beyond. At about that time a fad for octagonal houses (6), which supposedly improved their residents' health, was spurred by an eccentric phrenologist named Orson Squire Fowler.

# Religious Currents

Two of the numerous Shaker settlements in America were established in New York. In those self-sufficient villages the "Shaking Quakers," who practiced celibacy and reduced their communal life to fundamental values, remained a source of wondering interest for more worldly folk. The Shaker meetinghouse still stands at New Lebanon (1). In 1848 John Humphrey Noyes (2) established at Oneida, New York, a society of Perfectionists whose members held all property in common and practiced eugenic mating, communal care of children, and "complex marriage" within the group—each woman was the wife of every man and every man the husband of each woman. Oneida women adopted the Bloomer costume and cut their hair short (3). Of course, New Yorkers did not have to join a community to express religious sentiments. Church services and camp meetings, such as the one seen below (4), satisfied most people.

## Sing Sing

A house of a different order from Orson Fowler's octagonal house was built in the 1820s at Sing Sing on the Hudson River (1). It was a prison with one thousand cells, operated according to what at the time was considered a model system. Discipline was severe, enforced labor was hard and productive, silence was mandatory, confinement was solitary at night—and the hoped-for moral reform of the inmates seems questionable. Convicts, wearing the striped prison uniform (horizontal stripes on trousers, vertical stripes on shirts and jackets) were marched in rigid formation to and from meals (2). They were kept busy working in the prison's various shops—the hat manufacturing shop is shown below (3)—and on Sundays, they had the opportunity to examine their consciences under the watchful eyes of guards ranged along the walls of the prison chapel (4).

3

4

1

2

## The Crystal Palace

3

4

5

6

In 1853 the United States held its first world's fair at the Crystal Palace in New York City. The huge fair building, erected on the present site of Bryant Park, was made largely of glass and iron (1). In its central court stood a great equestrian statue of Washington (2), and in surrounding areas were gathered industrial and cultural exhibits from America and abroad, among them the safety appliance used in the Otis elevators made in Yonkers (3). Unfortunately, the "mighty Exhibition" was not a success and the enterprise went bankrupt. The palace building, though reputedly fireproof, went up in flames on October 5, 1858 (4). Commenting on the exhibits of American furniture at the Crystal Palace, Professor Benjamin Silliman of Yale College noted that the American public was "no longer contented with the plainness that was once satisfactory," adding, "A demand for decoration has arisen in every branch of manufactures. . . ." A well-appointed New York parlor furnished by the firm Bembe & Kimbel (5) demonstrates what Silliman meant. In 1856 the German immigrant John H. Belter, one of the best known of New York furniture makers, patented a laminating process in which six or eight thin layers of wood were glued together and pressed and steamed into curvilinear shapes, with additions of exuberantly carved embellishments. A table in that style (6) was a popular novelty of the midcentury.

# Upstate Cities at Midcentury

Before the Civil War a good number of the growing communities of upstate New York had been incorporated as cities. The largest and most flourishing of them, as earlier remarked, owed much of their importance to the magic touch of the canals and railroads that fingered their way through the crosscountry valleys of the state. In time those valleys came to serve as the most heavily traveled migration route in history. The natural highway to the West was an irresistible temptation to native and immigrant alike. The immense and continuous stream of migrants that coursed into the state, and through it, left a varied population behind as it passed along the way. Newcomers of various national origins mingled with the mixed stock of earlier arrivals, in cities and about the countryside. Today, a large proportion of New York's population remains clustered along that historic route; more than half its number are still either immigrants or of immigrant parentage. The cities illustrated on these pages are represented as they appeared around the middle of the last century—hardly more than two generations after the bloody frontier wars at the close of the Revolution, when much of the western region was still virtually a wilderness: (1) Oswego about 1850; (2) Rochester in 1853; (3) Buffalo in 1852; and—in the eastern, earlier-settled portion of the state—(4) Poughkeepsie in 1852 and (5) Albany in 1852.

4

5

## Syracuse and Utica

Near the shores of Onondaga Lake, Syracuse with its towering churches was settled in the years immediately following the Revolution and incorporated as a city in 1848, approximately the time when it was depicted in this richly detailed lithograph (1). Its favorable location on the Erie Canal stimulated industrial development. In 1841 an annual state fair began to be held at Syracuse, and the tradition has continued ever since. Utica (2), located along the Mohawk River and the Barge Canal, was settled in 1773 on the site of old Fort Schuyler and incorporated as a city during the Civil War, about a decade after the print here illustrated was published. On the high land in the extreme right background of the illustration is the building of the New York State Asylum for the Insane, opened in 1843 and the first institution in the state to care for the mentally disordered.

# THE WAR.

## Highly Important News from Washington.

### Offensive War Measures of the Administration.

### The President's Exposition of His Policy Towards the Confederate States.

## A WAR PROCLAMATION.

## Seventy-five Thousand Men Ordered Out.

On April 15, 1861, the New York *Herald* reported an appeal for 75,000 state militiamen from the North to meet the challenge of the South (1). Four days later, New York's crack parade unit, the Seventh Regiment, marched through the city streets in response to that appeal (2). Among the prewar volunteer militiamen were the exotically garbed Zouaves (3), patterned after the famous French fighting units and known for their elaborate and entertaining drills; they, too, soon marched down to the embarkation dock en route to Virginia. (There they quickly learned that their bizarre uniforms were not suited to military combat). Lincoln's call to arms became a matter of community pride; as the recruiting poster issued at Troy, New York, indicates (4), the names of popular leaders were exploited to stimulate local enlistments. One brigade of New York Zouaves was composed of members of the city's volunteer fire department; a French cartoonist rudely caricatured one of them fighting, not the Confederates, but thirst (5). Actually, at the time the government had little military support other than from such companies of energetic volunteers who uniformed themselves splendidly and drilled themselves effectively at their own expense, eager to parade on the slightest pretext. Such an outfit, the Suffolk Guard, was formed at the old seaport town of Sag Harbor as part of the New York state artillery (6).

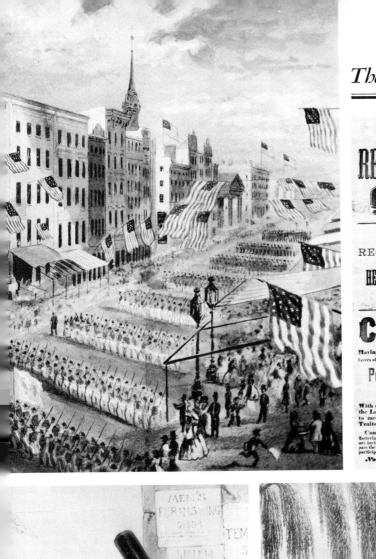

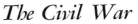

4

HO! FOR THE SUNNY SOUTH.

# RENSSELAER COUNTY REGIMENT OF VOLUNTEERS.

REGIMENTAL HEADQUARTERS,

69 FIRST STREET, TROY, N. Y.

# COL. W. T. WILLARD,

Having entered upon the duties and command of this Regiment, calls upon all Patriots and Lovers of their country to step forward at this most important crisis, in aid of their beloved country, in her efforts to

## Preserve the UNION, Protect the CONSTITUTION, AND TO EXECUTE THE LAWS.

With united efforts ... shall soon be in the a ... render aid to crush Rebellion, and restore the Laws to their protecting influence, enabling the Citizens of this great Republic once more to meet on terms of harmony and friendship, banishing the demon Rebellion, and ambitious Traitors who have brought this evil day upon us.

Company Officers for Six Companies, are actively in obtaining Volunteers at this moment, with flattering success. The other Companies will be organized immediately. YOUNG MEN of Character, Energy, and Capacity, are invited to come forward to fill up the unoccupied positions, and complete the organization. It is intended and desirable to pass the winter in a milder climate than our latitude affords. An early organization will do this, and enable the Regiment to participate in the operations now going on in the field of War.

.Nov. 18, 1861.

W. T. WILLARD, Col. Com'g.

5

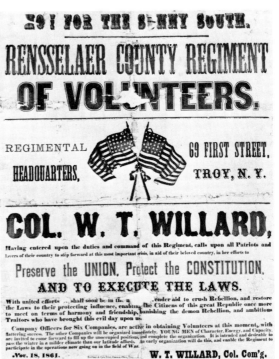

6

# The Home Front

In 1861 the government created the United States Sanitary Commission to care for sick and wounded soldiers and their dependent families. Funds to support such war relief work were provided by private contributions, and especially by Sanitary Fairs, such as one given at the city's Assembly Rooms in 1861 and depicted by Winslow Homer (1). A Soldier's Depot incorporating a hospital was also set up in New York with funds provided by the state (2). In September 1863, altogether unexpectedly, the czar of Russia's Atlantic fleet dropped anchor in New York Harbor (3). It was hopefully assumed that that "friendship visit" indicated Russian support for the northern cause at a critical moment in the war. Officers of the squadron (4) were welcomed in an enthusiastic parade along Broadway, which was attended by a vast concourse of curious New Yorkers. A few weeks later, to honor its guests further, the city staged the greatest ball and the most elaborate banquet the nation had ever witnessed (5). The morning after, that celebration was regretted; the bloodletting at Gettyburg and Chickamauga were still in the news, as hospital beds bore witness, and in cold daylight it hardly seemed the time for New Yorkers to engage in unrestrained festivity. Actually, it was learned much later, the Russian warships were refugees from their native ports, where they had been threatened with a blockade by a coalition of hostile nations.

2

# Draft Riots

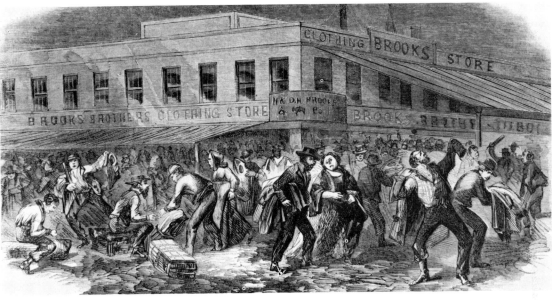

4

5

With the actualities of war, enlistments fell off in spite of the handsome bounties offered (1). The first nationwide military draft was authorized on March 3, 1863, and four months later the name of the first draftee in New York was drawn from a revolving drum (2). An almost festive mood marked the occasion. Almost immediately, however, New York was torn by the bloodiest riots in its history, disturbances bordering on revolution. What started as a protest by the poorer citizens against a law favoring those who could afford three hundred dollars to pay for a substitute, soon turned into an insurrection against the established order of things. The police in a counteroffensive (3) were ordered to "take no prisoners." For several days bloodthirsty mobs roamed the city almost at will, looting stores (above, (4), the Brooks Brothers clothing store is attacked); burning the Colored Orphan Asylum (5); and lynching blacks (6). Blacks were the main victims of that unparalleled violence; their willingness to work for lower wages threatened the jobs of the Irish immigrants who made up the majority of the mobs. The state militia and one Michigan regiment was rushed from Gettysburg to control the situation. Before order was restored, it is estimated that more than twelve hundred people were killed, eight thousand injured, and more than one hundred buildings burned.

6

1

2

New York played its ample part in providing the industrial muscle which in the end was a decisive factor in the ultimate victory of the North. The Novelty Iron Works, at the foot of Twelfth Street on the East River shore in New York City (1), had been making boilers and engines for river steamboats since 1836, as well as other kinds of heavy machinery. At this factory, the revolving gun turret for the iron-clad *Monitor* was improvised, making possible that ship's historic victory over the Confederate iron-clad *Merrimac*. Some three thousand cannons for the Union Armies were manufactured at the West Point foundry at Cold Spring. Dramatic paintings by the artist John Ferguson Weir show workmen at the foundry forging the shaft for a steamboat (2) and casting molten iron for an army gun (3). The federal blockade of southern ports proved that Europe could survive without southern cotton, but apparently northern wheat was still needed. A forest of masts almost choking New York's waterfront (4) suggests the enormous commerce in wheat that was funneled through the city's port. Between 1861 and 1863 the North supplied Great Britain with 40 percent of its wheat and flour.

## Postwar Corruption

The Civil War had provided northern speculators with ample opportunity to improve their fortunes, particularly if they abandoned all scruples in the process. Among the more infamous were Jay Gould (1) and Jim Fisk (2), who after the war joined with Daniel Drew in a successful scheme to strip the Erie Railroad of all its profits for their personal benefit. In 1869 the two plotted to corner the nation's gold market. The scheme was foiled but it resulted in an almost catastrophic drop in the stock market on September 24, "Black Friday," which threw the brokers and the public into panic (3). For brazen thievery of public funds none could match William Marcy (Boss) Tweed (4), Grand Sachem of Tammany Hall, leader of the infamous Tweed Ring, and a director of the Erie. Tweed and his henchmen robbed the public treasuries of amounts that may have been as high as $200 million before he was forced to flee the country. His ultimate downfall was precipitated by the merciless cartoons of Thomas Nast which began to appear in *Harper's Weekly* in 1869 and which exposed Tweed's venality in terms a wide public could quickly understand. Nast's most famous cartoon, published in 1871, shows the ravening Tammany tiger murderously at loose in the public arena while an imperious Tweed watches the slaughter with satisfaction (5).

## Industry Upstate

All along the central route of the canal and rail-road industries of varied sorts struck deep roots during the middle decades of the nineteenth century. In the 1850s Elisha Graves Otis established an elevator factory (1) at Yonkers to serve the newly high-rising city buildings and for lifting freight. He installed the nation's first safe passenger elevator in 1857 in a New York store, Lord and Taylor (2). By the 1870s elevator service had become a necessity, built into the construction of all the taller modern structures. In 1853 a young German immigrant named Bausch, associated with another young German named Lomb, established in Rochester what was to become and remain a firm famous for its optical instruments (3). Encouraged by the availability of low-cost coal, an abundance of glass-sand rock nearby, and ready rail connections to eastern markets, the Flint Glass Company moved from Brooklyn to Corning in 1868 (4). It, too, became famous for the diversity and quality of its products, ranging from utilitarian wares (including the famous telescope mirror made in 1937 for the Palomar Observatory at Mount Wilson in California—the largest piece of glass ever produced) to exquisite blown shapes, still made by individual craftsmen as glass has been made for centuries. George Eastman was born in Waterville, New York, and six years later moved with his family to Rochester. As a young man he there formed what soon was named the Eastman Dry Plate and Film Company (5). In 1888 he introduced a simple and inexpensive camera known as the *Kodak* (6), which he advertised with the slogan "You push the button; we do the rest."

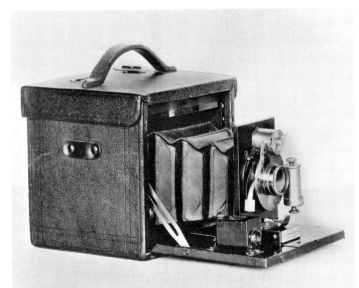

# Industrial Growth

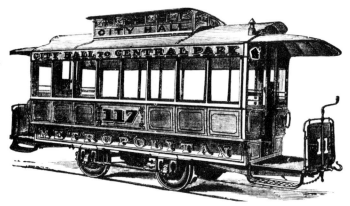

In the years following the Civil War, New York, along with the rest of the country, experienced a boom in manufacturing. Rapid growth in transportation accompanied the rapid, almost frantic growth of industry. In New York City, three hundred workers were employed in the factory of John Stephenson and Company, making street cars such as the one shown here (1), which was destined to travel between New York's City Hall and the newly laid out Central Park. Another New York City firm, First & Pryibil, manufactured woodworking machines, including a carefully designed woodcarving machine (2) capable of carving the "heads and other ornaments" that

4

5

adorned the ornate furniture so favored at the time. Along with richly carved furniture, many up-to-date homes of the post-Civil War period boasted decorative cast iron ranges. The one shown here was made in Troy (3). In Glen Cove, on Long Island, Duryea's Starch Works manufactured laundry and cooking starches in massive quantities, turning out up to forty-five tons a day. To serve the needs of industry, institutions like the Rochester Business University (5), a commercial school founded in 1863, promised a course of study that was "practical and so eminently thorough that the graduate is fitted to at once enter upon the business duties of life."

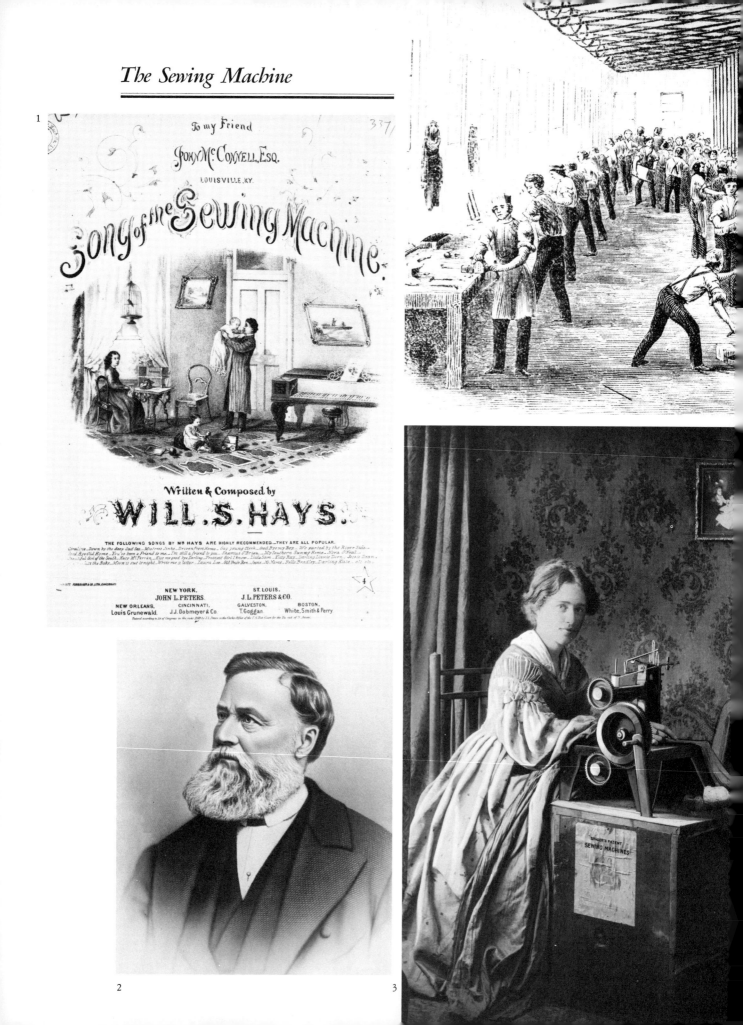

5

6

One of the most ancient forms of human art and drudgery—sewing—was mechanized on a large scale, providing a freedom for the housewife from time-consuming labor, which supposedly led to increased domestic felicity as she could spend more time with her children and husband (1). One of New York's most spectacular success stories had its beginning in 1851 when Isaac Merrit Singer (2) patented a sewing machine that was a great advance over the other existing models (3) and went into partnership with a New York attorney, Edward Clark. Within less than a decade these men had become the world's foremost sewing-machine manufacturers (4). The family "Singer," reported the *American Agriculturist,* was a tireless seamstress, "always at home when you want work done, never troubled . . . with aching shoulders,

nor with mumps, nor mopes." An advertisement appearing in *Frank Leslie's Illustrated Newspaper* (5) claimed that "any good female operator can earn with one of them one thousand dollars a year." Almost from the beginning the Singer Sewing Machine Company was selling more machines abroad than in the United States. In 1901 the company sought to boost its sales of one million machines a year with a folder advertising its "universal" operations (6). One share of Singer stock bought in 1863 for $200 had become worth about $36,000 by 1958. Singer himself, from 1834 to 1870, sired twenty-four children by five different women. He ended his life happily married and living in regal luxury on the Channel coast of Devon, England.

# The Burden Iron Works

An immigrant mechanic Henry Burden (1) became one of the great inventors of the nineteenth century, and one of New York's foremost industrialists. Under his management the Burden Iron Works at Troy (2) made that little city the horseshoe capital of the world. A machine invented by Burden could produce 3,600 horseshoes an hour, an output that gave the North a significant advantage over the South during the Civil War. In 1851 Burden had designed and installed an enormous water wheel (3), the most powerful of its kind in the world and one of the industrial wonders of the nation, with a capacity of 500 horsepower; the wheel used the Wynants Kill, with its steady flow of water from a chain of lakes east of Troy, as a power source. Even after its abandonment in 1900, the great wheel was revered as a monument to industrial progress, until it was dismantled and then scrapped, just before World War II. In 1862 the Burden company expanded to include a plant powered by twin blast furnaces (4). Some sixty years later the Republic Steel Corporation took over the blast furnaces, and the Burden Office Building, a handsome example of late Victorian commercial architecture (5). Little now remains of what was once an extraordinary example of American heavy industry.

4

5

1

2

3

4

Immediately beyond the bounds of its growing urban-industrial concentrates, New York remained a state of small villages and rural prospects. Early in the century Timothy Dwight, the president of Yale College, gazing over the New York landscape with its tidy hamlets and neatly cultivated fields, referred to the state as "a colony of New England." In the decades that immediately preceded and followed the Civil War, artists depicted the pleasant and picturesque aspects of that scene, which the passage of time has in many instances not yet obscured. About 1860 Smithtown, Long Island, appeared like a typical New England settlement, with its trim clapboard meetinghouse and dwellings facing the green (1). A decade or so later Constantine Herzberg rendered an idyllic view of Auburn (2), a town that in 1805 had chosen its name from Oliver Goldsmith's poem "The Deserted Village"—"Sweet Auburn, loveliest village of the plain." Joseph H. Hidley, the local taxidermist and woodcarver, painted a view (one of a number) of Poestenkill, in Rensselaer County, as it appeared in 1862 (3). Village life had its occasional and seasonal excitements, as when the circus came to town (4) or when the circuit court held its periodic sessions (5).

OVERLEAF: "Cider Making" by W. M. Davis recalls the vital part apple culture has played in the history of the state.

1

2

3

The nation's first factory-produced cheese was made in Oneida County in 1851. Around that time, New York farmers also pioneered the factory production of butter. At dairy factories, like the one above in Wightsboro (1), farmers brought in milk to be processed into cheese (2). The Dairy Man's Board of Trade had its home in Utica (3). Health standards for dairy products were unsatisfactory until the end of the nineteenth century, when new scientific advances, such as tuberculin testing of cattle, became widespread. The first pasteurized milk was distributed in New York City in 1893. New York has also been distinguished for its wines. As early as the seventeenth century a governor of New York claimed that the area under his administration could supply enough wine for all the dominions of the Crown. That prospect was hardly justified, but German, French, and Swiss settlers in later years did develop wines of good quality. In 1873, at the Vienna Exposition, New York State champagne won its first gold medal in Europe. One center of winemaking was Pleasant Valley. There, grapes were pressed in machines (4) and their juice, after fermenting, was bottled (5) as sparkling wine. In Long Island, a minor, rural occupation was slaughtering stranded whales which had been cast up by the waves onto beaches (6); the whales' blubber was rendered into lamp oil.

5

6

# In the Small Towns

Each county seat was a center of commerce, the site of the courthouse, and often the local center of culture. In Seneca County, the courthouse (1), built in classical architectural style, was located in a town named after the Latin poet, Ovid. The growth of small-town prosperity was stimulated by railroads. At Warwick in the resort area of Orange County, weary travelers had only to cross the road from the station to find lodging at the National Hotel (2). In Middletown, the Orange County Press (3) provided news, books, and job printing for local citizens. The Rathbun Merchant and Custom Mills (4) in East Pembroke was a small-scale operation compared to mills in nearby Rochester, but it was closer to the wheatfields. Throughout the state were prosperous farms, like that of David Odell in Tyre (5). They provided good business for the state's manufacturers of farm implements and for the products of the Tornado Windmill Company in Elba (6).

## Batavia

A tour along Main Street in the thriving market town of Batavia, midway between Buffalo and Rochester, would take the visitor past the monuments of commerce and culture that made the town a magnet for the citizens of Genesee County. At Number 53 Main Street, above the Turner and Jones meat and fish market stood the town's library and reading rooms (1). A little way down the street at Number 105 Main was the town's imposing opera house, only two years old at the time these views of Batavia were engraved in 1876. The opera house (2) boasted a fashionably ornate mansard roof, a balcony from which a band could serenade the populace, and that rare urban delight, a restaurant, on its ground floor. Diagonally across from it on Main Street was Kenyons (3), a small department store that sold crockery, groceries, and a variety of other items. Also on Main Street were a drugstore (4), a dry goods store (5), and a jewelry store (6) that sold clocks and picture frames as well. One local industry was that of John L. Foster, "manufacturer of fine carriages, buggies, and sleighs." Foster's two-story brick factory was located on State Street (7).

# Troy

The site of Troy, on the Hudson's east bank a few miles north of Albany, was originally a part of the Van Rensselaer manor grant of 1629. Early in the eighteenth century the property was acquired by Derick Van der Heyden, and until late in the century it was known as Van der Heyden's Ferry. Following the Revolutionary War, colonists from New England settled on that farm land and laid out a town there, which in 1789 was named Troy in the spirit of the classical revival of the period. It was one of thirty-one places in the United States that would take the name of that ancient city. There was hope that the hamlet might soon replace Albany as the head of navigation on the Hudson. The opening of the Erie Canal in 1825 stimulated the town's commercial and industrial growth, since it was the practical terminus of the canal, as well as of the Champlain Canal to the north. During the decades preceding the Civil War, Troy's industries flourished with the proliferation of railroads and the opening of new markets in the West. An arsenal on the west bank of the river supplied arms and ammunition to the northern armies during the war and the armor and machinery for the ironclad *Monitor* were made here. With the invention of the sewing machine in the 1850s, Troy's characteristic industry was launched—the manufacture of shirts, collars, and cuffs, and for years the city was the center of the laundry machine industry. The famous "female seminary," established by Emma Hart Willard in 1814, moved to Troy in 1821 and, with the Rensselaer Polytechnic Institute and other institutions of learning, helped give the city a fair reputation as an advanced educational center at an early date. This 1881 view from the north shows the city and the neighboring arsenal town of Watervliet across the Hudson. Factories and warehouses line the riverfront, from the region of the Green Island Bridge in the foreground down to South Troy. At right, parallel to the river, is an extension of the Erie Canal.

# Buffalo

From the beginnings of its settlement Buffalo has served as an important center of commerce with the principal American and Canadian ports on the Great Lakes. It was chartered as a city in April 1832. Within a few decades, its cobblestone Main Street was bustling with traffic (1). Horse-drawn trolleys carried passengers across a town that had grown enormously in a few years. By the time it celebrated the fiftieth anniversary of its charter, Buffalo, with its thirty-seven miles of waterfront (2) and its shipping canal (3), had become one of the largest grain-distributing ports in the United States—a point clearly made by the prominence of the huge storage elevators that lined its waterfronts (4). (The first grain elevator in the world was erected at Buffalo in 1840.) Provided with abundant railroad as well as shipping facilities and with nearby sources of power, the city attracted industry and other commercial activities which would eventually make it the center of the second largest metropolitan area in the state. In conjunction with its semi-centennial celebration, the cornerstone of the Soldiers' and Sailors' Monument (5) was laid in Lafayette Square. Grover Cleveland, then mayor of Buffalo and later President of the United States, was chairman of the executive committee for the occasion.

# The State Capitol

When Albany became the state capital in 1793, plans were laid for the construction of a new Capitol building. The structure (1) was first occupied in 1809, and although it served as the Capitol for the next seventy years, it was generally not considered adequate for its purposes. Among other criticisms, assemblymen habitually complained of "a dizziness in the head, accompanied by severe pain caused by the impure air thrown into the chamber" (2). In 1867, after much discussion, the Legislature appropriated money "towards the erection of a new capitol," which was not supposed to cost more than $4 million. After a series of bitter political disputes and a succession of shifting plans under a variety of architects, a portion of the structure was opened in January 1879. The $4 million limit had long since been substantially overspent. (In 1877 the then governor referred to the construction as a "public calamity, . . . without a parallel for extravagance and folly.") As it was finally completed (3), so that visitors could inspect all its wonders (4), New York's Capitol was easily the most eclectic building ever to be seen in the Hudson Valley. No historic style was neglected either in the interior or on the exterior; no improvisation seems to have gone untried in the straining for elegance and originality. The celebrated "million-dollar staircase," in which no design was repeated twice, itself cost more than its sobriquet indicated (5).

A small army of stonecutters was employed in the embellishment of the new Capitol, including an "elite" corps of carvers with special talents. Foliage and flowers—roses, clematis, trumpet vines, tulips, lilies, and the like—were gathered from the New York countryside to assure accuracy and authenticity in decorative motifs. An extraordinary assemblage of sculptured portraits peers down on the passing visitor. Among those so memorialized are James Fenimore Cooper (1), Walt Whitman (2), Harriet Beecher Stowe (3), Susan B. Anthony (4), Mollie Pitcher (5), Roger Sherman (6), Abraham Lincoln and U. S. Grant (7), along with representations of a raven (8), a log cabin (9), a raccoon (10), and a farmer at work guiding a plow drawn by a team of horses (11). Probably no other government building in America is so architecturally interesting, regardless of its aesthetic merits.

6

7

8

9

11

10

# *Westchester*

Westchester County in the second half of the nineteenth century was still a hilly, sparsely populated region of small villages and farms, with here and there, close to the railroad lines that had spread across the landscape, a factory or the suburban residence of a city businessman who commuted daily to the new Grand Central Station in New York. Yonkers (1), idyllically set along the Hudson River just north of New York City, was an exception; it was becoming a sizable city, its factories, most notable among them Elisha Otis's elevator works, attracting numerous immigrants to settle in the town. Northeast of Yonkers was White Plains, the county seat. An 1887 lithograph (2) shows the town from the south. At lower left are the railroad tracks and at lower right the Post Road leading to New York City. Many of the wealthy built mansions at White Plains and surrounded them with sprawling, carefully tended lawns. One such mansion was Rocky Dell Farm (3), the residence of a gentleman named J. Reynal. George H. Purser of Yonkers also gave his country estate (4) a suitably rural name, calling it Shady Dell. Another prosperous Westchester resident, William P. Van Rensselaer, situated his Italianate house (5) on Manursing Island, overlooking Long Island Sound at Rye.

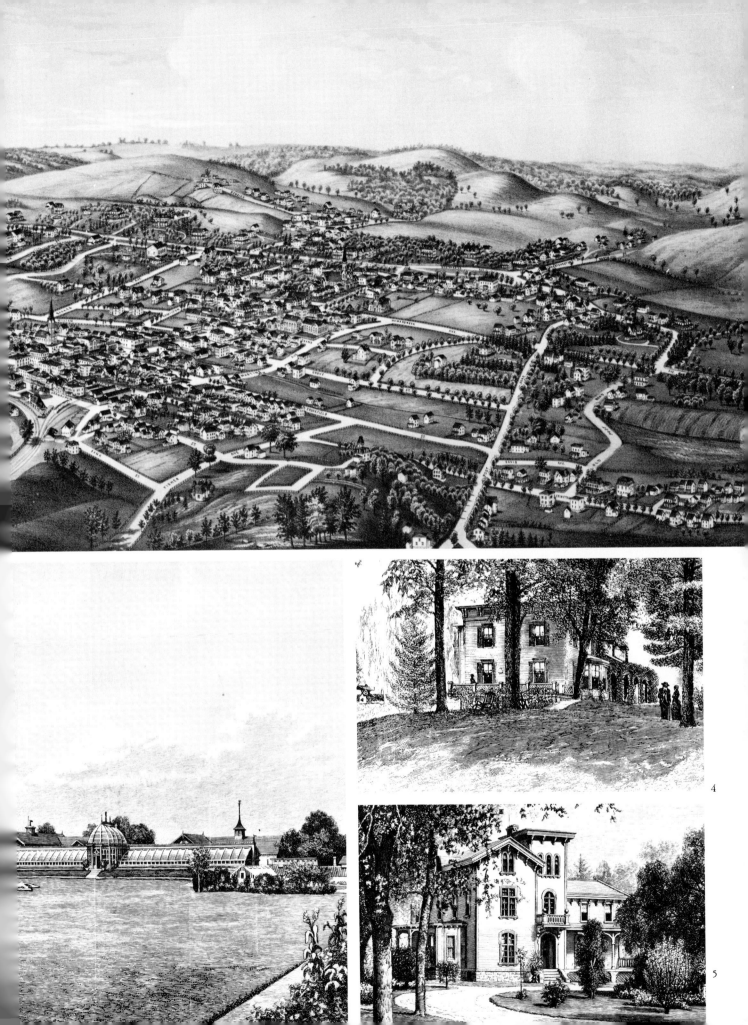

Schemes for the construction of an elevated railroad to relieve the congestion on New York's streets were broached as early as 1825, but the plans remained visionary until 1868. In that year *Harper's Weekly* reported that trial runs led "friends of the enterprise to hope that the problem of rapid and safe locomotion through the crowded streets of the city has been solved." The cars, it was reported, could be propelled "with little jar and oscillation, at the rate of fifteen miles an hour." Ten years later the line was formally opened. Above, one of its trains passes through Greenwich Village (1). It was quickly extended and new lines opened. The first trains were drawn by steam locomotives (2), one of which is shown on the new Sixth Avenue El in the 1870s (3). Sparks from their engines occasionally set fires in the streets below (4). A ride in the uncrowded accommodations of the elevated's pullman car (5) was an agreeable experience. The spreading system became a prominent New York landmark, with its stylish stations and platforms (6) and impressively engineered highways (7). At the end of the century the mayor declared that the public "should no longer be subjected to the . . . nuisances of noise, smoke, and flying cinders." Plans were made for electrifying the system.

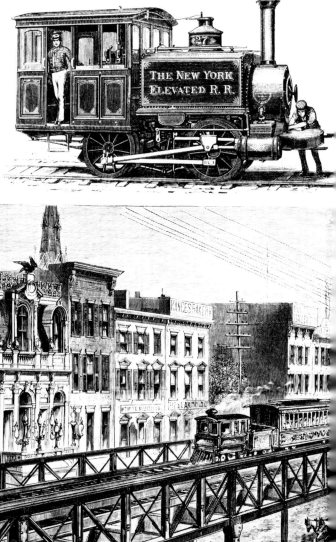

4

## Elevated Railroads

5

6

7

# The Brooklyn Bridge

For those who lived across the rivers from Manhattan, getting to and from work was often a frustrating trial. Ice, fog, and wind might delay transit by ferry for hours. However, building a bridge over even the relatively narrow East River seemed practically impossible. No part of that vital waterway could be blocked by piers, and the elevated roadway would have to be high enough to permit the safe and easy passage of the largest ships. A suspension bridge would be required, but the history of such bridges was marred by disasters. Yet in 1869 the legislature approved plans for a huge suspension bridge engineered by the most illustrious bridgebuilders of the day, the German immigrant John A. Roebling (1) and his son Colonel Washington Roebling. The great stone towers, rising 271 feet above water level, required massive underwater foundations, the construction of which was a formidable, perilous, delicate, and almost untried undertaking. It was accomplished by sinking giant caissons—inverted boxes—into place on the river's bed (2), then emptying them by forced air compression so that men could work within them. To connect the towers with sky-high wire cables was a prospect that terrified riggers called upon for the job (3). Early in the construction of the bridge, the senior Roebling died as a result of an accident on the job, and his son took over. Though he himself became incapacitated as a result of his work in the caissons, he continued to direct operations from the window of his sickroom (4). In 1883 the gigantic structure was completed (5), to be hailed as "the eighth wonder of the world."

## Croton Reservoir

Less than forty years after New York had constructed its first great aqueduct, that system was no longer adequate to provide the needs of the growing metropolis. Early in 1883 the legislature declared that "by the insufficiency of the city's water supply the people are deprived of the ordinary conveniences of domestic life, the public health is endangered, the security of property from fire is diminished, and the pursuit of commerce and manufactures is retarded." Once again the Croton watershed was tapped for the necessary new supply. Beginning at the southern extremity of the Croton Dam, then the largest dam in the world, a tunnel some thirty miles long was cut mainly through solid rock (1, 2) across a varied countryside (3) to reach the reservoirs that would serve the city. In the course of its transit the tunnel dropped hundreds of feet, crossed a river, and fed several storage reservoirs (4) with a total capacity of more than 8 billion gallons. The horseshoe-shaped conduits were planned to deliver an additional 250 million gallons of water daily, in the driest years, to urban consumers who, it was estimated, were using 100 gallons a day per capita, without heed for waste. The engineering construction, with its giant spillways (5), was not completed without payoffs and other forms of chicanery.

As early as 1844 William Cullen Bryant observed that commerce was "devouring inch by inch" the island of Manhattan. "If we would reserve any part of it for health and recreation," he said, "it must be done now." A full generation passed before the inspired design of the landscape architects Frederick Law Olmsted (1) and Calvert Vaux resulted in the completion of Central Park (2), after almost twenty years of dedicated thought and labor. The work of clearing the park site started in 1857. What had recently been a tangle of rock and swamp and squatter shacks, was gradually converted into what one early visitor called a "Paradise" which, with its bridges (3) and arched underpasses (4), its caves and lakes (5) and ramble, "would bear comparison with the boasted scenery of the old world." "Every foot of the park's surface," wrote Olmsted later, "every tree and bush, has been fixed where it is with a purpose." By 1873 between four and five million trees, shrubs, and vines had been planted. It had become what one highly responsible critic has called the "supreme American work of art." Beyond that, it provided a vital breathing place for the increasingly congested city. The park was completed in the centennial year of 1876.

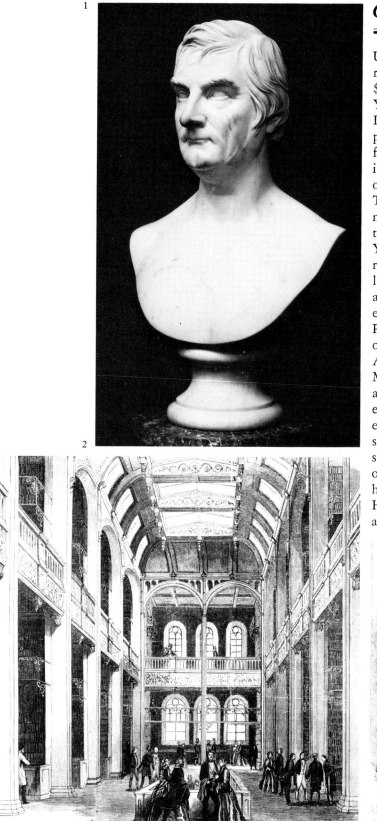

## Cultural Institutions

Upon his death in 1848, John Jacob Astor (1), reputedly America's richest man, bequeathed $400,000 to establish a public library in New York City. The original building of the Astor Library was opened in 1854 (2). In 1845 another prominent New Yorker, James Lenox, began to form a substantial library, which was incorporated in 1870 and installed in an appropriate building on Fifth Avenue at Seventy-first Street (3). Twenty-four years later, the two libraries were merged and, enriched with funds provided from the Samuel J. Tilden Foundation, formed the New York Public Library, one of the world's greatest repositories of books, manuscripts, prints, and related materials. In 1869 the New York legislature authorized the Central Park Commission "to erect, establish, conduct, and maintain in the Central Park" a museum of natural history and a gallery of art. That act led to the incorporation of the American Museum of Natural History and the Metropolitan Museum of Art. Plans for a great and prestigious museum in the city had earlier envisioned a splendid palace with one subterranean entrance leading through the park between colossal stone figures representing Ignorance and Superstition (4), but the museums were actually built on a more modest scale. Private openings of exhibitions at the Metropolitan (5) and the Natural History Museum (6) were formal social occasions, attracting a distinguished gathering.

# The Statue of Liberty

"Liberty Enlightening the World," the colossal copper figure better known as the Statue of Liberty, was conceived by the Alsatian sculptor Frederic Auguste Bartholdi and built in Paris during the 1870s and early 1880s (1). It was made of big sheets of hammered metal, shaped over plaster models (at upper right (2) the model of one arm and hand is shown), and welded over an iron framework engineered by Gustave Eiffel, whose tower would rise in Paris a few years later. Planned as a gift to the United States by the French people as a reminder of the friendly relations between the two countries, the colossus arrived a bit late for America's hundredth birthday, although the arm and torch were shown at the Centennial Exposition in Philadelphia. In 1885, when it was finished, it was shipped to America in 214 crates and put together on Bedloe's Island in New York Harbor, where it has stood ever since. The day of dedication, October 28, 1886, was the day "a hundred Fourths of July broke loose," reported the New York *Times*. Every type of vessel was hired to provide a close-up view (3). It was a misty autumn day, and a display of fireworks had to be postponed a few nights (4). Including its pedestal, the figure rose to a height of 305 feet, making it the tallest structure of the New York skyline at the time.

3

4

## New York Mansions

In 1869 Matthew H. Smith published *Sunshine and Shadow,* a bestselling book protesting the bitter poverty of those who lived in the slums virtually in the shadow of the elegant houses of those who had money to spare. The title page (1) illustrated the contrast with views of the Five Points slum and of the two-million-dollar mansion completed the year the book came out by Alexander T. Stewart, "the lucky immigrant." Two years later the prominent Wall Street broker Alfrederick Smith Hatch commissioned Eastman Johnson to paint a group portrait of three generations of his family gathered in the library of his commodious Park Avenue home (2). Those residences were but modest precursors of the much more elaborate mansions that were soon lining Fifth Avenue, notably those of various members of the Vanderbilt family. In 1884 William Henry Vanderbilt (3) held a press reception in the art gallery (4) of his recently completed house (5), "the most expensive private home in America." His sister lived in the adjoining building. The houses of William K. Vanderbilt (6) and Cornelius Vanderbilt (7) were built by the most prominent architects of the day, with increasing size and splendor, in styles that recalled the most opulent structures of the Old World. Not one of those princely structures remains standing today.

4

5

6

7

## 1

## Slums

In 1842 Charles Dickens wrote of the frightful horrors he witnessed in New York City's slums, where "men and women and boys slink off to sleep, forcing the dislodged rats to move away in quest of better lodgings." During the decades to come, such rookeries of degradation and pestilence worsened as the metropolis succeeded in cramming more people into less living space than had ever been accomplished by any community in the history of the world. A lodging center in the notorious Five Points district, pictured in a book published in 1872 (1), suggests that extreme of human compression. In the tenements (2), sorting rags from any possible source, including hospitals and "obscure chambers in which people have died of horrible and contagious diseases," provided marginal living for those who survived the work and

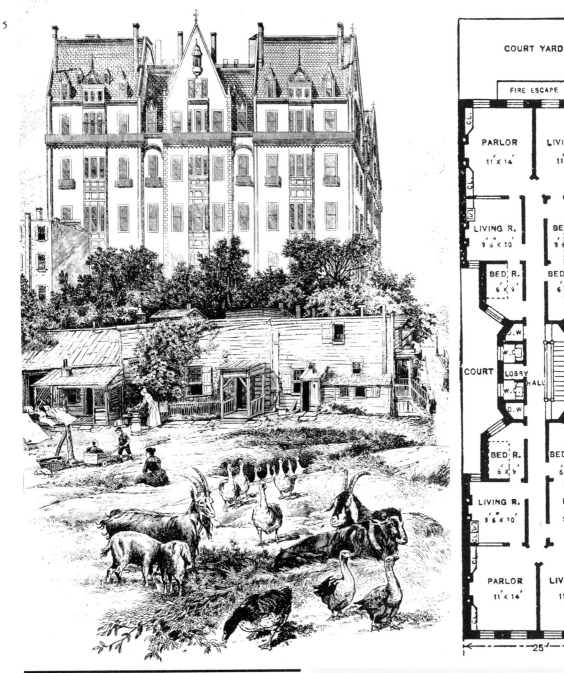

## 5

COURT YARD

FIRE ESCAPE

| PARLOR 11´ x 14´ | LIVING R. 11´ x 14´ |

LIVING R. 9´6˝ x 10´     BED R. 9´6˝ x 10´

BED R. 6´ x 9´     BED R. 6´ x 9´

D.W.   W.C.

COURT    LOBBY / HALL    COURT

W.C.   D.W.

BED R. 6´ x 9´     BED R. 6´ x 9´

LIVING R. 9´6˝ x 10´     BED R. 9´6˝ x 10´

| PARLOR 11´ x 14´ | LIVING R. 11´ x 14´ |

100´   87´   25´

exposure to disease (3). The health inspectors who made periodic inspections of tenement workrooms, "sweat shops" of human labor, held their nostrils to mitigate the stench (4). On the outskirts of the crowded sections of the city, the shanty town was hardly more salubrious (5). The passage of a Tenement House Law in 1879 did little to help. Old Law tenements with "dumbbell" floor plans (6) continued to house the poor in narrow, cheerless, and all-but-airless-and-lightless quarters, with two to four flats on a floor and public toilets on the landings. Such model tenements as were built under the auspices of the Improved Dwellings Association in 1880 (7) soon became slums themselves and set a general pattern of blight for future attempts to house those of meager means.

# *Huddled Masses*

Between 1881 and 1900 almost nine million immigrants entered the United States, principally through the port of New York. Almost nine million more arrived in the first decade of the present century. Every arriving ship carried its full burden of alien newcomers (1). Earlier and smaller waves of immigration had brought people largely from the northwestern perimeters of Europe—English, Irish, Germans, and Scandinavians. Now in increasing proportions came central and eastern Europeans. Like the Ruthenian (2) and Swedish (3) immigrants shown here, they came garbed in native costumes that seemed totally unfamiliar and picturesque to Americans of older stock, and they were joined by another, less well-known, group of migrants, southern blacks, who came by train and ship (4) seeking a better life in the North. For many years immigrants to New York were received at historic Castle Garden (5). In 1892 a much larger depot was opened on Ellis Island, where immigrants were registered, questioned, and given health examinations to supplement the health checks they had undergone before leaving Europe and aboard ship (6). A significant volume of this torrential flow of incipient Americans was shunted into the already crowded slums of the city to make their way out as best they might. By 1890 New York had half as many Italians as Naples, as many Germans as Hamburg, twice as many Irish as Dublin, and two and a half times as many Jews as Warsaw.

217

Both in New York City and upstate, immigrants clustered together, establishing their own neighborhoods where street signs, foods, costume, customs, and even architectural styles evoked memories of the old countries which they had only recently, enthusiastically left. Along the narrow, twisting streets of New York City's Chinatown (1), immigrants clung to their traditional Oriental style of dress. Not far away was Hester Street (2), one of the centers of the metropolis's increasingly populous Jewish quarter. The Hebrew letters on the store sign advertise wine and brandy for the holiday of Passover. Nearby, on Mulberry Street (3), the store signs, and even one of the official United States Government Post Office signs, were in Italian. Here, as on Hester Street, pushcarts and outdoor stands offered food for sale. New York offered a free education to all immigrant children, hastening the process of Americanization. A photograph by Jacob Riis, who documented the immigrants' struggle to adapt to their new surroundings, shows a classroom in an East Side grammar school during the 1890s (4). Beginning in 1892 immigrants entering the United States through the port of New York were screened at offices on Ellis Island (5).

218

2

# Huddled Masses

## Better Living

In the last quarter of the century, as people began to swarm into New York City, problems of congestion mounted. To cope with the needs of those who were neither poverty-stricken nor very rich, as early as 1870, apartment houses, or "French flats" as these novel expedients were called, were erected, such as the seven-story structure designed in New York in 1881 (1). These were, in effect, high-class tenements in which could be rented suites of six rooms and a bath, plus the splendid convenience of a dumbwaiter. Within a relatively few years such accommodations were commonplace. One of the more enduring of those creations, which still survives, was called the Dakota Apartments (at right, 2), because West 72nd Street, where it was built in 1884, fronting on Central Park, was considered as far from the center of the city as the Dakota Territory. Apartment-house living provided up-to-date plumbing like the bath tub shown here (3)—central heating, elevator service, and other conveniences, although not as many as those which appear in an 1883 satirical drawing (4). May 1 was the traditional moving day in New York when tenants moved from one flat or house to another (5). For children, rich or poor, the roofs of New York provided a fine playground (6). Eventually, splendid roof gardens, planted with full-size trees, would be seen atop many apartment buildings.

*THE FRENCH FLAT OF THE VERY NEAR FUTURE EVERYTHING ON THE PREMISES*

*IN THE KITCHEN*

*IN THE PARLOR*

# Eating Out in New York

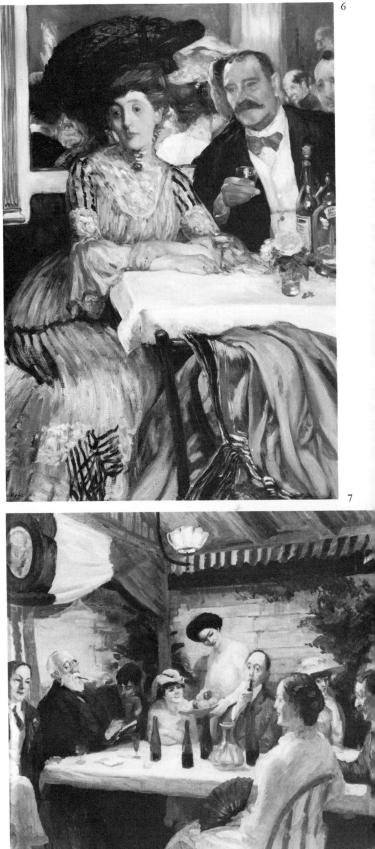

As cities grew in size, people obliged to work at increasing distances from their homes needed eating places where lunches could be had at modest prices, and, usually, in a hurry. New York had short-order restaurants at least as early as the 1820s and they have proliferated ever since. By the 1870s the quick-lunch counter (1) had become commonplace. Childs' became the most popular chain of low-priced restaurants; its tile and marble establishments were city landmarks in the early decades of this century (2). With the advent of the automat (3), as reported by *Harper's Weekly* in 1903, the service of lunch or dinner took only about one minute. Those with more leisure and larger means could dine elegantly at Delmonico's fashionable restaurant (4) or give supper parties after an evening's entertainment at the Waldorf-Astoria (5). *Chez Mouquin,* painted by William Glackens (6), pictures a couple in a French restaurant that was popular among artists, writers, and men-about-town. In 1910 Glackens's fellow artist John Sloan painted a typical gathering for dinner at Petitpas, another French restaurant popular among writers and artists (7). The author and critic Van Wyck Brooks sits at the far left, next to John Butler Yeats, Irish painter and father of the poet William Butler Yeats.

224

# Merchandising

The Civil War period saw the development of the department store in America. By the 1870s such establishments were offering merchandise of almost every description under one roof, frequently displayed in palatial surroundings. Lord & Taylor opened its new store on Broadway in New York City in the spring of 1871 (1). Here, in addition to a wide variety of yard goods, as promised in an 1871 advertisement (2), the rare shopper who could afford it could consider the purchase off the sales floor (3) of a suit with narrow silk ruffles "most mysteriously convoluted," and exorbitantly priced at $275. Those with less expensive tastes could choose from a stock full of other possibilities, or patronize one of the numerous other department stores that attracted shoppers in New York City in the years following the Civil War. In rural areas the traditional country store continued to serve local customers, and to function as a gathering place where gossip could be freely traded (4), but throughout the state almost every community of size and pretension boasted at least one department store. Factories that produced dress goods and associated articles were operating from one end of the state to the other. In Jamestown, dress goods were manufactured, and Troy became famous for its shirts and collar factories (5).

4

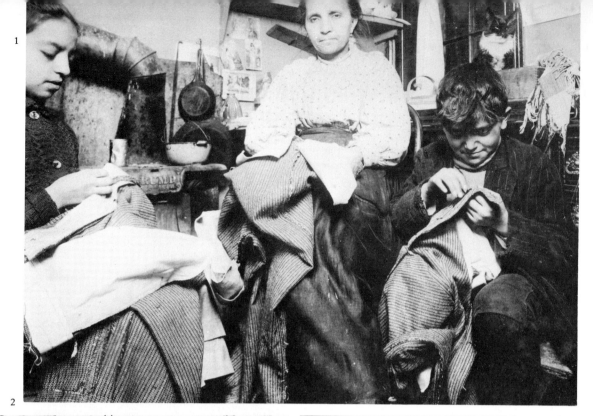

For a century past, garmentmaking has ranked among the most important industries of New York. Until the early 1900s, work was commonly farmed out to the lowest bidder and the handwork was performed either at home in a crowded tenement room (1, 2) or in so-called sweatshops (3), in either case under appalling conditions and with minimal pay. Small children, as well as adults, were enlisted to carry home and to move from place to place partially completed garments in need of finishing (4). A manufacturer might subdivide the making of a coat, for example, into as many as thirty-nine different operations, any one of which required only rudimentary training and experience and could depend upon low-grade labor. Much of this labor was recruited from among the poorer immigrants who were swarming into the city and the state in such vast numbers, and who were relatively defenseless against exploitation. "The average American woman," reported one observer in 1915, "is the best dressed average woman in the world, and the Russian Jew has had a good deal to do with making her one." At far right a group of Jewish garment workers gather on New York's East Side to protest inequities within the industry. It is important to note that, despite their immigrant background, these men are thoroughly Americanized in their own dress (5).

# The Garment Industry

3

4

5

227

# Recreation

Long before Brooklyn was incorporated as a political component of New York City, the sandy beaches on its ocean front at Coney Island had been converted into a unique amusement area where hundreds of thousands of refugees from the metropolis came in summer to escape the congestion and heat of city streets, to ride along the ocean front (1), to enjoy the attractions of its exotic and sometimes lurid sideshows, and to bathe in the ocean. On summer Saturday afternoons, other city residents crowded Grand Central Station in New York, going off for trips to the country (2). In the Catskills, vacationers inspected the curious rock formations and waterfalls (3) or took their ease on the sunny balconies or shady porches of hotels like the Mountain House at Lake Mohonk near New Paltz (4). Saratoga, seen at right during Race Week (5), retained its popularity. Winter resorts also attracted sportsmen, like the toboggan slide on which the citizens of Albany disported themselves in 1886 (6).

OVERLEAF: At Steeplechase Park in Coney Island, visitors in 1903 could enjoy a gondola ride on the Venetian Canal, a trip on a roller coaster, or an exciting ride on the giant seesaw, atop its tall tower.

5

6

During the closing decades of the last century New Yorkers joined with other Americans across the nation in an active interest in and pursuit of sport. The rise of the popularity of baseball was phenomenal; it had become the national game. By the 1880s thousands of spectators were paying to watch New York's professional team perform against its rivals at the Polo Grounds (1). By the 1880s also, an American version of football had been developed and systematized as a largely inter-collegiate sport, with its greatest early success in eastern colleges. On October 19, 1889, in upstate New York, the college teams of Rochester and Cornell squared off in a contest before an informally gathered audience of modest size (2). Cornell won, 124—0. The wealthy New York publisher, sportsman, and bon vivant James Gordon Bennett introduced polo to America in 1876; the game quickly became popular among athletic young men who could afford it and who performed at such places as the Rockaway Hunt Club and Jerome Park (3) before a restricted group of fashionable folk. Golf of a sort had been played in New York since the eighteenth century. The St. Andrews Golf Club, organized in 1888 at Yonkers, New York, by John Reid and his neighbors, reflected a new-born interest in the game (4). At least at one time in the 1880s, New Yorkers could witness bullfights with genuine toreros, and presumably fighting bulls, too (5).

233

# Women in Sports

Women took to sports with gusto as the century waned. On the opening day of the Ladies' Athletic Club at Camp Washington in Staten Island, New York, in the early summer of 1877, they displayed their proficiency in archery (1), among other outdoor exercises that notably included lawn tennis (2), a game which rapidly came into favor as an "elegant and pleasant pastime" about that time. Tennis was imported into the United States from Bermuda in 1874 by Miss Mary Ewing Outerbridge of Staten Island. It had been invented in Great Britain just a few months earlier. Indoors, bowling competed with tennis and croquet as a popular and fashionable diversion, hobbled though these ladies also were by their attire (3). In 1895 Mrs. Charles S. Brown won the first Women's Golf Championship Tournament at Meadowbrook, Long Island, with a chivalrous male companion to retrieve her putts (4). As nothing had before, the mutual participation in sports brought about a free, wholesome companionship of men and women; and nothing did this more effectively than the fad for bicycling that swept New York as it did the rest of the country in the late nineteenth century. No other form of outdoor exercise had won such an enthusiastic following; bicycling played a large part in liberating women from the bondage of Victorian fashions in clothes and behavior. On country roads or on Riverside Drive in New York City (5), the sexes mingled in their pursuit of this new-found happiness.

235

## Vassar and Cornell

1
2

4

3

Land Scrip No. *5291* for "One Quarter Section."

## Colleges for Agriculture and Mechanic Arts.

ACT OF CONGRESS, JULY 2, 1862.

For State of *New York*

**Whereas**, in pursuance of the Act of Congress approved July 2, 1862, entitled "An act donating Public Lands to the several States and Territories which may provide Colleges for the benefit of Agriculture and the Mechanic Arts;

The State of *New York* has accepted the Grant provided by the said act, and under the same, has consequently a legal claim to *One Hundred and Sixty Acres*, not locatable by the State itself, but liable to transfer, and may be located by the **Assignees** of said **STATE**, according to assignment, attested by two witnesses, in the form on the back of this instrument; the location by Assignees in satisfaction of the claim above mentioned, to be made in virtue of a regular Series of Scrip, a part of which is this:

Land Scrip No. *5291* for "One Quarter Section."

**Therefore be it known**, That this **SCRIP**, when duly assigned and attested by two witnesses, under such authority of the said State as the act of the Legislature thereof may designate, may be surrendered at any Land Office of the **UNITED STATES** in satisfaction of a location of "One Quarter of a Section" or for any quantity in one legal subdivision less than "One Quarter Section; where such location is taken in full for "One Quarter Section"—the location to be restricted to *vacant public lands* subject to entry at private sale at $1.25 per acre, **MINERAL LANDS EXCLUDED**; and whilst the aggregate location of all the claims under the said act may be taken in any of the **TERRITORIES** without limitation as to the quantity located in any one of them, yet, in virtue of express limitation in the Statute, "not more than One Million Acres" of the total aggregate Scrip issue under said act can be located within the limits "of any one of the States."

**Given** under my hand and seal of the Department of the Interior on the *twenty third* day of *July* A.D. 186*3*, and of the Independence of the United States the *Eighty Eighth*.

Recorded, *Vol. '9 Page 41.*
*Jno. Edmunds,* Commissioner of the General Land Office.

*W. T. Otto* Acting Secretary of the Interior

The first great college for women in the United States opened its doors at Poughkeepsie in 1861. The celebrated institution was made possible by the generous benefaction of Matthew Vassar, son of an English immigrant, who had immensely prospered with his "ale and oyster saloon" and especially his brewery. First called Vassar Female College, in 1867 it was renamed simply Vassar College. Its massive main hall (1) was designed by the noted architect James Renwick. Its initial enrollment of 353 young women from many different states taxed the capacity of even that ample structure. When it was installed in the 1860s, Vassar's observatory (2) was the fourth largest in the nation, and classes in astronomy, supervised by the famous Maria Mitchell, were a feature of the college's program. The majority of the young ladies were from well-to-do and prominent families, and the annual commencement ceremonies were events of social as well as academic interest (3). The first American college to provide co-education was Cornell, which was chartered in 1865 and opened its doors at Ithaca in 1868 (4). It too had been made possible largely by private financial support, in this case from Ezra Cornell (5), a founder of the Western Union Telegraph Company. Additional aid came through the Morrill Act, passed by Congress in 1862, which offered grants of public lands (6) to help establish colleges of agriculture and mechanical arts in the separate states.

Illuminations

The Amphitheatre

A Rustic Seat

C. Graham, del.

The Museum

Hall of Philosophy

# The Chautauqua Movement

*In the Outlet.*

*Fairpoint Landing*

*Sectional view of Pyramid*

*Bird's-eye view of Jerusalem*

The Chautauqua movement originated on the shores of Lake Chautauqua in the northwest corner of New York State in the summer of 1874, for the purpose of improving Sunday School teaching, organization, and management; but it soon developed into a large-scale summertime colony with an expanding program of religious, educational, and recreational activities that attracted large numbers of participants. Literature, science, music, arts and crafts, physical education, and other subjects were studied with earnest interest amid idyllic surroundings. The program marked a beginning of what we now call the summer school, and a new start in the continuing education of adults. In 1878 home-study courses were instituted and won wide audiences numbering many thousands, who constituted what has been called America's first book club. The very considerable returns from publishing helped to keep the institution in the black. The lakeside "campus," shown here in an 1880 magazine illustration, rapidly developed to accommodate the community's pursuits. There was a large lecture hall (upper left), which was sometimes filled four times daily; over the years Chautauqua speakers included the most prominent figures of the day, including Presidents of the United States. There was also a hall of philosophy recalling the Parthenon (bottom center); a museum (lower left); a miniature model of Jerusalem (lower right); and a sectional reproduction of an Egyptian pyramid (right center). To house visitors, a hotel, cottages, tents, and boarding-houses sprang up. Excursion steamers (center) plied the attractive lake with boatloads of appreciative customers. Within two or three decades hundreds of local assemblies sprang up in America, more or less imitating the Chautauqua plan and often calling themselves *chautauquas*.

# Olana

1

2

3

Easily the most picturesque architectural monument that has survived in the Hudson Valley from the 1870s is Olana, the "Persianized" mansion built by the notable American landscapist Frederick Edwin Church (1) on the crest of Mount Merino overlooking the river just south of Albany. Church sketched the house about 1875, shortly after its completion (2). Having acted as his own architect and decorator with advice from Calvin Vaux, "I can say," he remarked, "as the good woman did about her mock turtle soup, 'I made it out of my own head.' " Taking advantage of the ample resources he had culled from his painting, he wove into the design of his exotic residence ornamental themes drawn particularly from Near Eastern models (he had traveled extensively in the Near East)—"so far as the climate and the requirements of Western civilization permitted." Among those requirements was "modern" plumbing (3, 4). From all angles Olana presents a different and colorful spectacle (5, 6) and its windows and balconies command views of the Hudson River and the Catskill Mountains, panoramic vistas which Church often painted (7). To Church, Olana was "the Center of the World." And, he added, "I own it." It is now owned by the Olana Historic Site, and is opened to the public from May to November.

## 7

For more than a century and a half the Catskill Mountains have made a rich and varied contribution to the history of New York. To this day the imaginative visitor to this area can sense the abiding presence of Rip Van Winkle (1) and his troop of small folk, as Washington Irving described them. Those forested highlands became the favorite haunt of the Hudson River school of painters, as witnessed here by Samuel Colman's view of Storm King (2), just north of West Point. The fabled gathering place of storms, Storm King serves as a weather signal to neighboring residents. Because of its large stands of hemlock trees, whose peeled bark was used to make tanning fluid for curing hides (3), some of which were bought from as far away as South America, the Catskills helped make New York the greatest leather-producing state in the 1840s. Then and in the years that followed, the Catskills also became a prime vacationland, dotted with picturesque inns, to which the Kaaterskill Railway (4) and stagecoaches provided easy access. In the late 1870s a hotel-building mania swept the area. The Hotel Kaaterskill (5), opened in 1881, was probably the most elegant, most fashionable, and most talked-about of those pretentious structures. From his farm in the Catskills, barely eighty miles from New York City, the naturalist John Burroughs (6) wrote lyrical essays about the wilderness world—books that were bestsellers in their time and that have made his cabin there a shrine in our own days.

1
2

3

4

The wild and majestic beauty of the Adirondack Mountains attracted artists as well as nature lovers, woodsmen, and others from an early date. In 1858 a distinguished party that included Ralph Waldo Emerson, Louis Agassiz, William J. Stillman, and other learned and companionable persons, held an idyllic meeting at the "Philosophers' Camp" near Follansbee Pond. Stillman recorded the occasion in a painting (1). Longfellow refused to attend when he heard that Emerson would carry a rifle. "Then," he predicted, "somebody will be shot." No one was. The next year in another oil painting, Eliphalet Terry depicted a clearing in the forest near Minerva where a family named Baker had settled several years earlier (2). (The land was later purchased for the North Woods Club.) Winslow Homer first went to the Baker farm in 1870 and in the thirty-odd years to come, on his frequent visits to the Adirondacks, he recorded aspects of the life of the sportsmen, loggers, and hunters and fishermen who frequented that wild area, in a succession of superb watercolors and oils. In such paintings as "Hound and Hunter" (3), "Huntsman and Dogs" (4), "Old Friends" (5), and "Adirondack Lake" (6), he pictured those men, whom he never identified, who faced the wilderness of the northern woods with the self-reliant confidence born of the pioneer spirit. Homer was not a New Yorker, but his Adirondack scenes contributed to the desire of Arnold Bennett, the English dramatist and novelist, to come to America to see his work. "They were beautiful," Bennett wrote of Homer's work; "they thrilled; they were genuine America; there is nothing else like them."

1

2

Shortly after the Civil War the substitution of wood pulp for rags in the manufacture of newsprint vastly stimulated lumbering activities in the Adirondacks (1). For some years New York led all other states in the production of pulpwood and paper products, an eminence that seriously threatened its magnificent stands of trees. The extension of railroad lines into the central area of the mountains during the 1870s (2) not only facilitated the cartage of lumber but also lured vacationers to regions earlier known only to trappers, anglers, hunters, and lumbermen. Where the railroads did not reach, stagecoaches (3) brought visitors to such elegant rustic resorts as the Prospect House, with a capacity of five hundred guests, on Blue Mountain Lake in the backwoods, which was opened in the summer of 1882 before some of its attendant buildings were completed (4). That establishment was extravagantly hailed at the time as a structure of unequaled magnitude and magnificence; its restaurant was famed for its excellence; through its halls (5) thronged expectant refugees from the growing congestion and pressures of urban life. In the early summer of 1878, the *Utowana* (6), first of a long series of vessels of the Blue Mountain and Raquette Lake Steamboat Line, made its maiden trip. For decades, until hard-surfaced roads were introduced, such conveyances plied the inland waterways.

3

4

5
6

# The Telephone

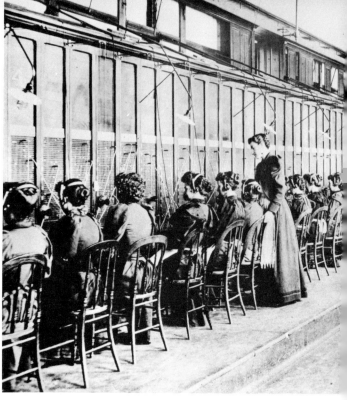

New York's first telephone directory was issued in October 1878. No numbers were listed for the 252 entries, since calls were made by name. Five months later the first city telephone exchange was opened. The switchboards each held a dozen wires. Boys served as the first operators (1) but they were soon replaced by girls, who proved better suited to the job (2). Within a few years the telephone evolved from a curious electrical novelty to a practical convenience and then to a necessity. Without it the huge concentration of people in office buildings and the acceleration of business activity would have been impossible. The English visitor Arnold Bennett was impressed by "the efficiency and the fearful universality of the telephone," which startled and frightened "the backward European in the United States." Transmission wires began to spread into an almost solid copper canopy over such streets as Broadway (3). In 1884 the legislature passed a law requiring that "all telegraph, telephone, and electric light wires and cables" must be "removed from the surface of all streets or avenues" and put underground (4) before November 1 of the following year—a very considerable operation. That same year the first long-distance telephone line in the world was constructed between New York and Boston, an extension of the medium's range that was dramatized in 1892 when the inventor Alexander Graham Bell helped celebrate the opening of the World's Columbian Exposition in Chicago by uttering from New York the first words ever spoken over the wires between the two cities, as officials of the telephone company watched with satisfaction (5).

248

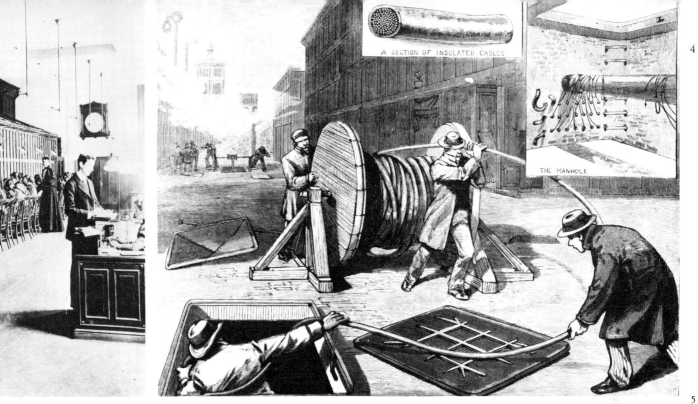

A SECTION OF INSULATED CABLES

THE MANHOLE

# *Electricity*

5

6
7

Laying the Electrical Tubes

In 1880 the electric arc light invented by Charles Francis Brush was tested by New York City officials (1) and found acceptable. It was first used in the city for lighting a section of Broadway. With that improvement one could not only read a newspaper in the street at night (2) but, as use of the device was extended, one could also swim at Coney Island at night in its bright glare (3). Within a few years arc lighting had become relatively common on major streets, and the tempo of city life after dark accelerated (4). Almost at the same time, Thomas Alva Edison invented an incandescent lamp (5) that was more suitable for indoor use. In 1881 he moved the headquarters of the Edison Electric Light Company from New Jersey to New York City. That same year the board of aldermen authorized the Edison company to lay tubes, wires, conductors, and insulators and to erect lampposts in all the streets of the city, subject to a fee of one cent per linear foot for each street (6). Edison's first electric lighting station, on Pearl Street (7), was one of the wonders of the metropolis, attracting almost universal attention. The current from the giant dynamos was turned on September 4, 1882, with fifty-nine customers for the service, including the New York *Herald,* the *Times,* and Drexel, Morgan and Company.

1

2  3

4

In 1886 Thomas A. Edison moved his growing electrical machine works from New York City to a factory at Schenectady (1). With its expanded facilities the company was prepared to satisfy the increasing demand for dynamos (2) and other necessities of the electrical world. At the time, dozens of firms throughout the country were competing for control of sources of electrical power and for the manufacture of equipment to complement it. In 1889 most were consolidated into a major national industry, the Edison General Electric Company (3). At Rochester, a central station of Edison's competitor, Charles F. Brush, was providing service for both arc lights and incandescent lamps in large quantities, as well as producing power for shops and industries (4). As early as 1880 Edison had been associated with the celebrated New York designer Louis Comfort Tiffany, who was quick to capitalize on the advantages of electric lighting. With the newly invented bulbs, now for the first time in history the source of light could be pointed downward, as well as up, as Tiffany handsomely demonstrated with his fashionable appliances (5). At Corning, New York, J. Hoare and Co. produced richly cut glass bulbs for the new electric lamps (6).

# Energy

The most spectacular natural feature of New York State is Niagara Falls (1). Almost three centuries ago Father Louis Hennepin first described this imperial cataract in a book that ran to thirty-five editions in four languages before it went out of print; during the course of those editions, his reports of the "vast, prodigious Cadence of Water" increased its height more than three times. H. G. Wells, who visited the falls some two hundred years later, admired them less for their sheer beauty than for their almost infinite potential as a source of power. As much untapped power was daily flowing over Niagara as was contained in all the coal mines throughout the world during the same period. In the 1890s a good portion of that power was harnessed to practical service as electrical energy. As shown in two pictures at lower left (2,3), an artificial waterfall was created by digging a pit about a mile above the falls, connected with the river by a canal (marked A) and leading through pipes (B) to water turbines (C) that in turn, through a metal column (D), powered an electric dynamo (E). The wasted water was discharged through tunnels (F, G) into the river below the falls, whose scenic grandeur was thus in no way defaced. In 1890 an international Niagara Commission had been established in London to determine the most efficient form of turbines and of power transmission, resulting in the selection of a design for the turbines (4) by a Swiss firm. Five years later, the water power of Niagara Falls was harnessed to three generators, each developing 5,000 horsepower, and within a few years, Niagara power was being "piped" to consumers almost two hundred miles away from the source. Wells looked forward to the day when all the "froth and hurry" of the falls, "dying into the hungry canals of intake, should rise again in light and power, in ordered and equipped and proud and beautiful humanity, in cities and palaces and the emancipated souls and hearts of men."

4

## The Trolley Car

To keep up with the pace of life generated by the new sources of electrical energy, vehicles swifter than horsecars were needed to quicken traffic. By the close of the nineteenth century, the landscape became overlaid by trolleycar lines, along some of which a traveler might travel by interconnecting services for hundreds of miles at a stretch. Efficient dynamos and cheap current had revolutionized urban and suburban transportation. In 1906 promoters dreamed of a Chicago–New York Air Line Railroad, an interurban electric line that would speed passengers between the two cities aboard one hundred-mile-per-hour trains much faster than steam locomotives (1). The scheme never materialized, but other lines prospered. At the end of the century a roadbed was laid and wires strung for the Oneonta, Cooperstown and Richfield Springs Railway (2), which began operation over a fifty-three-mile rural New York route in 1900. About that time an interurban trolley station of the International Railway at Lockport, New York, complete with baggage section (3), accommodated passengers headed for other upstate places, including Niagara Falls. The trolley car became an irresistible vehicle for pleasure jaunts. At Elmira, New York, a double-decker trailer (4) carried excursionists to an amusement park; in New York City cars crowded with passengers were whisked off to Coney Island (5). The spread of trolley networks encouraged suburban development, but having accomplished so much within fifty years, the electric trolley eventually gave way to the automobile.

At the turn of the century, upstate New Yorkers found ample opportunity for recreation, some of it as energetic as jumping rope (1), apparently a pastime for grown women in Cherry Valley at the time, and some quite relaxed, as the boating couple on the Susquehanna River demonstrates (2). Bathing in nearby Otsego Lake was a pleasure easily come by for residents of Cooperstown (3). A few years earlier one editor expressed fears that such ladies' bathing costumes might set off "a riot of personal license between the sexes which leaves nothing to the imagination," but, as it proved, he need not have worried. More decorous by far, croquet was a game that was played everywhere (4). The well-dressed croquet party shown here was photographed on Main Street in Cooperstown around 1885. Clothes of a more patriotic and more distinctive nature were worn by six teenage girls, inmates of a Cooperstown orphanage called the Susan Fenimore Cooper Foundation and participants in a patriotic pageant (5). Those girls, and indeed all the upstate New Yorkers depicted on these pages, led lives far different from those of their city counterparts, whose recreational opportunities were severely limited. Even the Vanderbilts in their mansions on treeless Fifth Avenue had to rely on potted palms for contact with the beauties of nature.

# *Life at the Turn of the Century*

During the last decade of the nineteenth and the first decade of the twentieth century New Yorkers were living in what was for them modern times (as people always have). For us, looking back from the uneasy vantage of the nuclear age, the pace of their lives—of those who lived outside the bustling urban precincts, at least—seems almost unbelievably gentle, the pursuit of their occupations measured and relaxed. In 1907 tree-shaded North Avenue in the small Dutchess County town of Fishkill (1)—now only a mile or so away from an interstate superhighway— appeared as a haven of tranquility, like other such "nice" neighborhoods in towns throughout the state. Looking across the town of Cherry Valley in Otsego County from a slope of the lovely

orchard countryside, as the ladies and gentlemen of the 1880s shown in the accompanying photograph (2) were privileged to do, gave ample reason for contentment. About 1890 the saloon in Canandaigua offered solace of a different sort (3). In honor of the New Year season, whisky was being sold at one dollar a quart, and "Oysters in Every Style" were available. At the First National Bank of Cooperstown (4) the tellers apparently had time for neighborly chats with their customers. Women, whose work is proverbially never done, could make light of some of their chores by gathering in congenial groups to sew, knit, and embroider, as three generations of the Olcott and Dakin family are shown doing in the 1880s in a comfortable Cooperstown home (5).

## Literary New York

New York has spawned a host of literary celebrities and attracted many more from other areas. Toward the end of his tragic life, Edgar Allan Poe (1) came to New York to write briefly for the New York *Sun* and to compose "The Raven," a poem that created an overnight sensation. Herman Melville (2) was born in New York in 1819 and returned there after his extensive seafaring to write out his days until he died in 1891. Like Melville, Walt Whitman (3) was a New Yorker of mixed Dutch and British stock. The iconoclastic critic H. L. Mencken did not hesitate to call Whitman "the greatest poet that America had ever produced." In the 1880s William Dean Howells (4) left the editor's chair of the prestigious *Atlantic Monthly* and moved from Boston to New York, which he found "lordly free" in its artistic tolerances. Willa Cather (5) came to New York, where she wrote her sympathetic and knowing classics of the Nebraska plains. On the other hand, Henry James (6) and Edith Wharton (7), both well-born New Yorkers, quit the local scene to exchange its "vulgarities" for the greater sophistication they found largely in European circles. In 1895 Stephen Crane (9) wrote *The Red Badge of Courage* while he was working as a freelance journalist in New York. He later claimed he got his "artistic education" on Manhattan's Bowery. The list of authors who produced their best work in New York is endless. In our own day, Carl Carmer (8) recreated the history of the state and the lore of its people in a series of books and stories written with affection, humor, and erudition.

263

# *Skyscrapers*

1

The Tower Building, completed in 1889, was New York City's first steel-skeleton structure (1). It was greeted with some skepticism by an apprehensive public, although four years earlier Chicago had blazed the way for such innovative skyscraper architecture with the Home Insurance Company Building. However, by 1894 *Harper's Weekly* reported that New Yorkers were getting quite accustomed to such lofty constructions. Within four years of that observation Manhattan's profile had already begun to take on its chaotic, jagged, ever-changing, and preposterously beautiful outline of towering buildings (2)—a shifting graph of man's busiest dreams over years to come.

4

3

The race for ever-taller buildings was on. In 1901 the St. Paul and Park Row buildings were represented as "the two tallest structures in the world" (3). Only the sky seemed to be the limit, as a visionary scene—"King's Dream of New York," which appeared in a book of New York City views published in 1908—clearly suggested (4). Because of its odd triangular structure, the Flatiron Building, erected in 1901–1902, was for several years the city's most famous skyscraper (5). In 1913 that distinction was securely gained by the Woolworth Building (6), a 792-foot-high "Cathedral of Commerce" designed by Cass Gilbert and for almost twenty years the "highest in the world."

5

6

265

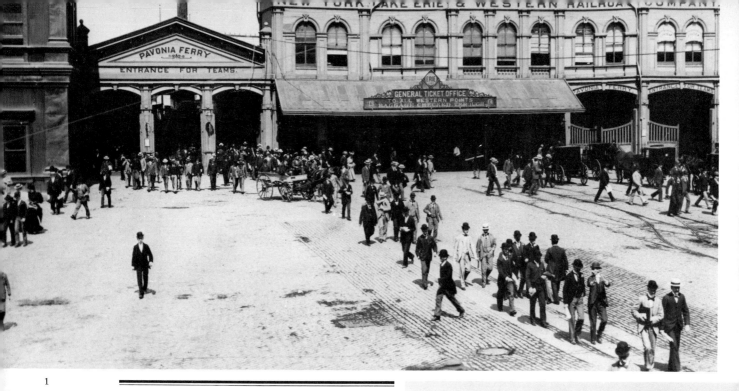

1

The spread of trolleycar lines had made it possible for people to get out of cities and back in again more quickly and cheaply than ever before. A new type of working person, the commuter, multiplied prodigiously. Before the end of the last century New York City—notably Manhattan Island—swelled and diminished each morning and evening in gigantic daily pulsations of population as the commuters arrived and left. In 1898, according to *Harper's Weekly,* the number of people who commuted to Manhattan every day was greater than the entire population of Cincinnati. Some 100,000 came by ferry from New Jersey (1), and as many by train (2), bridge, and ferry from Brooklyn. Even more came by trolley and train from Westchester and Connecticut. To facilitate the traffic a new Grand Central Depot (3, 4) had been constructed in 1871, at Forty-second Street, serving the New York Central & Hudson River, the New York, Harlem, and the New York & New Haven railroads. Although the building was much enlarged in 1899, it still proved inadequate, and was replaced by the present structure, completed in 1913 (5). The New York Central had acquired subsurface title to lands north of the terminal along Park Avenue, where the tracks and the trainyards were put underground (6). There they still run beneath the huge office buildings and expensive apartments that came to line that thoroughfare.

2
3

# Commuters

## 5

# Automobiles

1

With the turn of the century New York succumbed to the craze for automobiles. The first automobile taxi service in New York City was instituted in 1898 with electrically propelled vehicles shown here outside the Metropolitan Opera House (1), driven by young college men who knew something about electricity and storage batteries. Around 1900, a single auto was photographed venturing out onto Fifth Avenue (2); at right center in the photograph, it appears almost dwarfed by the horse-drawn traffic. In 1905 Smith & Mabley, Inc., opened a salesroom and garage on upper Broadway, "the Finest Motoring Shop in the World" (3), where imported turnouts were displayed. New York State laws prohibited driving over ten miles an hour in congested areas, and over twenty on the open road; but on special speedways daredevils raced against one another (4) to win the cup donated by William K. Vanderbilt, Jr. As late as 1913 the hazards of motoring remained common enough to provide the subject of a popular song (5). However, by the time of World War I, when the accompanying photograph was taken showing Fifth Avenue draped with patriotic banners, motor vehicles crowded city streets (6). By then, Sunday driving had become popular and stables had been converted into garages, as was E. J. Christ's garage, photographed at Hempstead in 1907 (7).

3  4

6

7

269

## *The Stock Exchange*

In December 1865 the New York Stock Exchange moved into a new building on Broad Street near the corner of Wall. It was, observed the New York *Times*, "one of the finest temples of Mammon extant." About 1879 the artist William H. Beard pictured the structure in the background of a satirical painting illustrating the frenetic struggle between the "bulls" and the "bears" of Wall Street (1). For all the financial wizardry it might display, the exchange continued to be shaken by periodic crises and panics when trading got out of hand. One of the most severe occurred in the fall of 1907. Bank suspensions and failures followed throughout the country. Wall Street was thrown into complete confusion and overflowed with clamorous, worried depositors (2). *Pearsons Magazine* of London ran a photograph which the publication termed "the first successful attempt to catch in the camera the great gambling scene on the floor of the New York Stock Exchange" in all its disarray (3). Only the wonder-working, autocratic genius J. P. Morgan, then over seventy years old (4), managed to avert a complete collapse of the market by commandeering $27 million to lend to member firms that were in trouble. Then, on October 29, at a time when it was virtually impossible to borrow money, he scribbled his initials on the notepaper of his library (5), announcing his underwriting of the $30 million bond issue that saved the city of New York from bankruptcy and helped bring the panic to an end.

5

# Ash Can Art

New York City has long been a focal center of artistic activity in the United States. Soon after 1900 a group of painters known as the "Eight," or the "Ash Can School," congregated there. They painted few ash cans, there were more than eight of them, and they formed no school. They might rather be called "New York realists," for in general their aim was to find and forthrightly represent subjects in the daily life of their urban milieu, however commonplace these might be. (A number of them had been artist-reporters for newspapers, trained to catch the appearance of things exactly as they happened.) Thus, John Sloan chose to depict McSorley's celebrated bar, an "out of the way retreat for appreciative ale drinkers" (1). With complete candor, George Luks, known to his intimates as "Lusty," painted "The Old Duchess" (2), a portrait of a picturesque and bibulous character once well known around Jefferson Market. In 1902 Robert Henri, the leader of the Eight, painted a winter night scene on West 57th Street (3), as a few years earlier Everett Shinn had sketched a similar scene on Broadway (4). In 1901 George Bellows painted "Cliff Dwellers," a view of the New York slums (5). His earlier canvas, "Stag at Sharkey's" (6), had as its subject a typical scene in the athletic club across the street from the studio of his teacher Robert Henri.

5

6

# Attention!

**ALL MALES** between the ages of 21 and 30 years, both inclusive, must personally appear at the polling place in the Election District in which they reside, on

## TUESDAY, JUNE 5th, 1917

between the hours of 7 A.M. and 9 P. M. and

# Register

in accordance with the President's Proclamation.

Any male person, between these ages, who fails to register on June 5th, 1917, will be subject to imprisonment in jail or other penal institution for a term of one year.

## NO EXCUSE FOR FAILURE TO REGISTER WILL BE ACCEPTED

**NON-RESIDENTS** must apply personally for registration, at the office of the County Clerk, at Kingston, N. Y., AT ONCE, in order that their registration cards may be in the hands of the Registration Board of their home district before June 5, 1917

Employers of males between these ages are earnestly requested to assits in the enforcement of the President's Proclamation.

Signed,

BOARD OF REGISTRATION
of Ulster County
E. T. SHULTIS, Sheriff
C. K. LOUGHRAN, County Clerk
Dr. FRANK JOHNSTON, Medical Officer

1

After German U-boats had torpedoed a number of American ships without warning and Americans sailing on British ships had lost their lives, an outraged America entered the war on April 6, 1917. Although one senator warned that there would be bloody anticonscription riots as a consequence, on May 18 Congress passed a draft bill, and signs and broadsides appeared throughout the state—the one shown here was issued at Kingston (1)—urging men to register for the draft. Throughout the state, men of practically every national origin registered. In New York City, draftees prepared to parade proudly up Fifth Avenue on their way to training camps (2), and eventually to entrain for ships that would take them to the front in France (3). To arouse support for the Liberty Loan, a bond issue authorized by Congress in April 1917, large rallies were held in American cities. The popular moving-picture actor Douglas Fairbanks came to Wall Street to exhort audiences that packed the street to buy the bonds (4). At Mineola, workers in Long Island's infant aircraft industry assembled airplane motors for use in France (5). By November 9, 1918, it was all over "over there," and delirious celebrations were staged in New York and in all cities across the land. The crowd shown here is celebrating Armistice Day on Wall Street (6) beneath a shower of confetti.

In 1918, when it was "over over there" to most doughboys returning from their "great crusade" in Europe, the Statue of Liberty looked sweeter than ever, as Rollin Kirby's drawing suggests (1). The spirit of self-denial and regimentation induced by war efforts made it possible to write the Eighteenth Amendment, prohibiting liquor, into the Constitution; it was ratified in 1919. Another of Kirby's drawings caricatured that repressive measure (2). The famous corner saloon soon gave way to the speakeasy, in New York (3) as in most other communities across the land, and thirsty lawbreakers were rampant. When, the next year, all women in the United States were given the right to vote, thanks were due in good measure to the pioneering movement for women's rights that years earlier had been led in and from New York by Elizabeth Cady Stanton and Susan B. Anthony (4), and by their militant followers in the state (5). After a brief recession, the nation's economy strode ahead at a quickening pace in the postwar years. For most of the twenties the "Street" enjoyed such a bull market as had rarely if ever been seen before. A dauntless optimism led to unrestrainable speculation. To keep up with the pace of trading, brokers (6) at times worked all night and conducted their business on the curb.

ANNOUNCING A NEW WEEKLY MAGAZINE

# THE NEW YORKER

HE NEW YORKER will be a reflection in word and picture of metropolitan life. It will be human. Its general tenor will be one of gaiety, wit and satire, but it will be more than a jester. It will not be what is commonly called radical or highbrow. It will be what is commonly called sophisticated, in that it will assume a reasonable degree of enlightenment on the part of its readers. It will hate bunk.

As compared to the newspaper, The New Yorker will be interpretive rather than stenographic. It will print facts that it will have to go behind the scenes to get, but it will not deal in scandal for the sake of scandal nor sensation for the sake of sensation. Its integrity will be above suspicion. It hopes to be so entertaining and informative as to

While the stock market climbed to giddy heights during the twenties, New York City's dandified and grossly irresponsible mayor, "Jimmy" Walker (1), set a miserable example for his fellow citizens by devotion to his personal pleasures and a sublime indifference to the public weal. Greenwich Village in downtown New York City was the twenties' celebrated Bohemia and a nationally recognized artistic center. The tolerant amorality of a village party was captured in a contemporary painting by Wood Gaylor (2). Edna St. Vincent Millay (3) was the district's poet-in-residence. In 1925 the *New Yorker* started publication of its weekly issues (4), which have reached a national audience for more than half a century. The decade of the twenties had opened on a promising note when, in 1920, George Herman ("Babe") Ruth (5) hit 54 home runs (and 59 the next year) to catapult the New York Yankees into sudden prominence. But the decade's greatest hero was the aviator Charles Lindbergh, who flew alone across the Atlantic and on his return home received a tumultuous welcome in New York (6). In the dark autumn of 1929 the stock market collapsed with a thunderous crash that had worldwide reverberations (7). It was the end of an era.

## WORST STOCK CRASH STEMMED BY BANKS; 12,894,650-SHARE DAY SWAMPS MARKET; LEADERS CONFER, FIND CONDITIONS SOUND

| FINANCIERS EASE TENSION | Wall Street Optimistic After Stormy Day; Clerical Work May Force Holiday Tomorrow | LOSSES RECOVERED IN PART |
|---|---|---|
| Five Wall Street Bankers Hold Two Meetings at Morgan Office. | Confidence in the soundness of the stock market structure, notwithstanding the upheaval of the last few days, was voiced last night by bankers and other financial leaders. Sentiment as expressed by the heads of some of the largest banking institutions and by industrial executives as well was distinctly cheerful and the feeling was general that the worst had been seen. Wall Street ended the day in an optimistic frame of mind. | Upward Trend Start• With 200,000-Share Order for Steel. |
| CALL BREAK 'TECHNICAL' | The opinion of brokers was unanimous that the selling had got out of hand not because of any inherent weakness in the market but because the public had become alarmed over the steady liquida- | TICKERS LAG FOUR HOURS |

The Great Depression suddenly and violently shattered the almost mystical notion that America's growing prosperity was heaven-sent and boundless. The nation was unfamiliar with and unprepared for suffering on the scale that soon resulted. An English observer noted that the stock market crash "outraged and baffled" the millions who took it as "an article of faith . . . that America, somehow, was different from the rest of the world" and immune from want and need. The grim realities were unmistakable as unemployed men and women desperately took to selling apples on the streets of New York or waited in breadlines (1) for handouts of food. In both urban and rural regions poverty was severe. The children at left were photographed playing in the South Bronx (2); the girl at lower left was photographed on a porch in Albany County (3). As a result of the Depression New York's governor, Franklin D. Roosevelt, was elected to the presidency in 1932. In 1936 three young working men were photographed in front of campaign posters urging his reelection (4). Depression did not dry up the mainstream of American optimism. In 1931 the Empire State Building was completed, 1250 feet high with 102 stories—then and for long the tallest building in the world (5). That same year ground was broken opposite St. Patrick's Cathedral for the construction of Rockefeller Center (6). On May 1, 1939, John D. Rockefeller, Jr., ceremoniously drove the final rivet into the steel of this extraordinary complex of buildings which completely transformed a substantial midtown area and remains one of New York's most impressive architectural monuments.

# Fiorello

New York City has an annual budget in the billions, larger than that of New York or any other state. The city has hundreds of thousands of employees on its payroll. In all its complexity and its problems, the city has repeatedly been termed "ungovernable." Its most efficient, most controversial, and most happily remembered mayor was Fiorello Henry La Guardia (1), the son of an Italian immigrant, who came to office in 1933 and served for twelve consecutive years. The "Little Flower," as he was affectionately called, made superb appointments, cracked down on crime and police corruption, obtained a new city charter, reformed the civil service, and gave New York the most efficient and incorruptible administration man could remember. He seemed to be always on the spot, everywhere the city faced problems. Wearing a fireman's helmet, he was quickly at the scene of major conflagrations. Thus he appeared to direct firemen at a rehearsal of air-raid precautions (2). To dramatize his campaign against crime he took ax in hand to smash slot machines shortly after he took office (3). He played the part of a store clerk to demonstrate the Food Stamp Plan (4), and with an instinctive flair for public relations he undertook to read the Sunday comic strips to children over the city's radio station. One of the high points of his tenure came with the opening of a gigantic world's fair on land in Flushing Meadow, Long Island, that had been reclaimed from a tidal swamp. The exposition, dedicated to "The World of Tomorrow," was dominated by the theme center, the seven hundred-foot-high Trylon, and the Perisphere, two hundred feet in diameter (5).

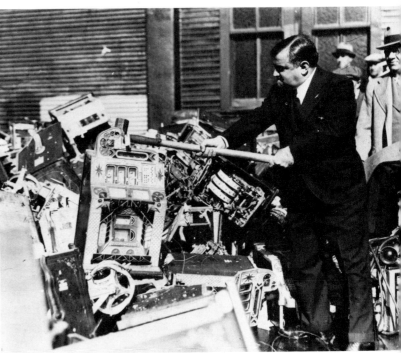

1
2

3

# World War II

"The World of Tomorrow" was still on display at Flushing Meadow when, with the outbreak of war overseas, the world of the immediate future took on a completely different cast. A dismaying number of Americans accepted Hitler's ideology. In New York's Yorkville neighborhood, heavily populated with people of German descent, militants goose-stepped through the streets in Nazi style to advertise their leanings (1). Nevertheless, Americans prepared for war. In 1940 Congress authorized the nation's first peacetime conscription, and remarkably cheerful draftees were put on trains headed for training camps (2). Millions of New Yorkers bought war bonds, raising a substantial part of the money needed by the federal government. New York children joined another drive to collect aluminum scraps to feed our growing war machine (3). At the outbreak of the war, the total output of American airplane factories was less than six thousand units a year. In 1940 the President asked the industry to gear-up to an annual production of at least fifty thousand planes. In 1944 production totaled almost one hundred thousand planes. On August 14, 1941, the Curtis-Wright Corporation opened another new plant in Buffalo, where pursuit and combat planes of various types were soon rolling off the assembly lines (4). All the major cities of the state became vital centers for the production of war supplies. One-half of the troops that set out for Europe and Africa, and one-third of the supplies supporting the allied war effort left through the port of New York (5).

5

2

In the twentieth century New York State has been well served by its governors. The Progressive Era that started with Theodore Roosevelt's inauguration as governor in 1899 (1) and reached a climax during the administration of Charles Evans Hughes (2), curbed public utilities, regulated public service corporations, improved the civil service, and evolved the nation's first worker's compensation laws. Then, starting with the election of Alfred E. Smith in 1918 (3), New York had a continuous stream of capable governors of the highest character. Smith, a product of New York City's Lower East Side, of Irish parentage, and a Roman Catholic, overhauled the organization of the state government, reformed its budget, and established a forty-eight-hour maximum work week. He was succeeded by Franklin Delano Roosevelt (4), who, as the Great Depression deepened, inaugurated imaginative measures of public relief. Next, Herbert H. Lehman, son of German-Jewish immigrants (5), almost single-handedly pushed through a series of progressive labor laws. In 1942 Lehman was succeeded by Thomas E. Dewey (6), a man of great administrative talent who appointed many professionally qualified department heads, created the State University, and initiated a major highway program. His successor, Averell Harriman (7), established the first office of consumer affairs, among other accomplishments. Then Nelson A. Rockefeller (8), shown here with his successor Malcolm Wilson (at right), built one of the most complex and socially advanced state governments in the United States.

## Governors

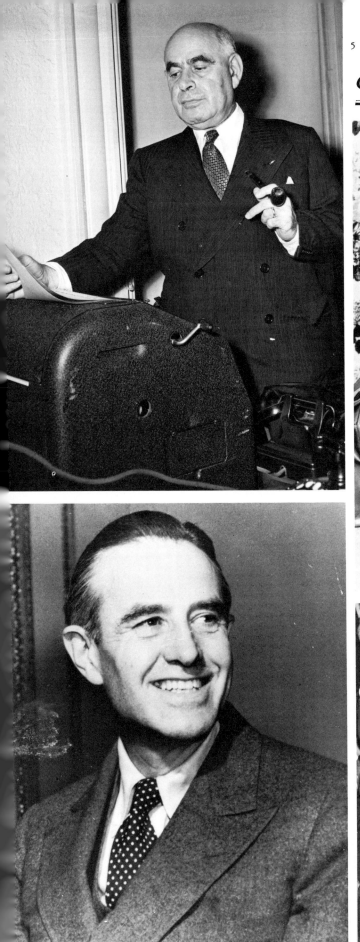

# Highways

With the advent of automobiles, opening adequate highways became a great pioneering adventure. The state began taking over the building and maintenance of the main roads within its boundaries and helping counties and towns construct and care for minor, local routes. On Grand Central Parkway in Queens, a cloverleaf interchange was built alongside Flushing Bay (1). A great thruway (2) to serve the most densely populated and richest industrial area of the state was undertaken in 1942 and opened to motorists a dozen or so years later. Now named the Thomas E. Dewey Thruway, this extraordinary artery stretching for more than four hundred miles across the state, from New York City to Buffalo, follows the historic route paralleling the Hudson River, the Mohawk River, and the Erie Canal. In 1921 New York and New Jersey jointly established the Port of New York Authority with jurisdiction over transportation facilities within twenty-six miles of the Battery at the tip of Manhattan Island. One of the agency's early acts was the construction of the extremely graceful George Washington Bridge between Manhattan and New Jersey, with (as later improved) its two-level, fourteen-lane roadways (3). Another was the building of two automobile tunnels, the Holland and the Lincoln (4), underneath the Hudson. A system of bridges linking the counties of Manhattan, Bronx, and Queens was erected in 1929–36 by the Triborough Bridge and Tunnel Authority. One of them, the Bronx Whitestone Bridge, is shown here (5). The most spectacular achievement of this agency has been the Verrazano-Narrows Bridge, spanning the Narrows between Brooklyn and Staten Island (6).

3

4

5

6

# Air Traffic

4

5

An airport in Newark, New Jersey, first served the New York metropolitan area, but it soon became overcrowded. To supplement it, La Guardia Field was built in 1935–1939 in Queens. That was in the days before routine transatlantic service had been established, when seaplanes, called "clippers," were still being used for long flights over water (1). In the postwar years, crossing the Atlantic by air was reduced from a challenging stunt to a routine, as hundreds of crossings were scheduled each week. Traffic control at airports like La Guardia became a demanding problem as planes crowded the airways and runways (2). By the 1940s the combined facilities of Newark and La Guardia were insufficient, and in 1948 a new, larger airport was opened at Idlewild in Jamaica Bay on Long Island. Since renamed John F. Kennedy International Airport, the station, frequently enlarged (3), serves more than 20 million passengers a year, along with an enormous traffic in air freight. The Port of New York, with its varied facilities under the control of the New York Port Authority, has become the airline crossroads of the world. The Authority also maintains helicopter services to quicken local transport. The heliport above juts into the East River off Lower Manhattan (4). Intrastate air traffic is handled by such operations as Allegheny Airlines, the country's largest "local carrier" (5).

The waterways of New York constitute one of the state's important commercial assets. Since the Hudson River channel has been deepened by thirty-two feet, Albany can be reached by large oceangoing vessels the year around (1). Grain elevators at the water's edge in Albany and in Buffalo (2) play a major role in the American grain trade. In northern New York the need was long felt for a canal that would carry large ships around the rapids on the St. Lawrence River. In 1959 the St. Lawrence Seaway, built by the Power Authority of the State of New York in cooperation with Canada, was dedicated (3) in the presence of Queen Elizabeth II of England, shown speaking, and of President Eisenhower, seen seated at right. Its twenty-seven-foot-deep channel (4) was planned to enable oceangoing vessels to reach the industries of Rochester and Buffalo, as well as other cities in the Middle West bordering the Great Lakes. New York's canal system extends more than eight hundred miles throughout the state; the Barge Canal connecting the Hudson with Lake Erie accommodates vessels large enough to travel the Atlantic Ocean (5).

# Waterways

New York constitutes one of the most productive dairy areas in the nation, and grazing cattle can be seen throughout the state's rural landscape (1). Almost half the income of all New York's farms comes from dairy products, principally from milk, which is carried to market by railroad tank car and truck from virtually all corners of the state. More revenue comes from the making of butter and cheese; above right, a worker prepares Chateaugay cheese (2). New York also produces vast crops of hay. What does not go to feed cattle is threshed for seed, for which the state is noted. A good many of New York's numerous farms (about fifty thousand were counted in the 1970 census) are devoted to apple production, and orchards like the one shown here (3) can be seen throughout Dutchess and Columbia counties. The wines made in New York are deservedly acclaimed throughout the country. Between 1955 and 1970 the state's vintners trebled their production and more than quintupled their output of champagne. In an average year, production amounts to about 21 million gallons of wine, far less than is produced in California where the grape-growing season is much longer, but more than any other state. Along the shores of Keuka Lake (4), and on sunny slopes elsewhere in the state, grapevines cling to their trellises.

# Modern Industry

The largest single industrial employer in New York State is the General Electric Company which, from its beginnings in the last decades of the nineteenth century, has expanded to include major plants in Utica, Auburn, Syracuse, and Schenectady, among other production centers. At Schenectady the main plant is a city in itself, with its hundreds of buildings and miles of streets (1). Alco, a leader in the design and manufacture of four-cycle diesel engines (2) like the one shown above, has its headquarters in Auburn. Across the state, near Buffalo, the huge plant of the Bethlehem Steel Company at Lackawanna on the shores of Lake Erie (3) is one of the most important of the operations that make the area by far the principal steel production center in the state—and one of the great industrial areas of the nation. The power shovels opposite (4) are shown preparing to unload a shipment of iron pellets from a cargo vessel docked at Lackawanna. The International Business Machine Corporation, which for years has had its center at Endicott, near Binghamton, in the southern tier, has constructed additional large plants in Poughkeepsie (5), Oswego, and Kingston. Among the state's mining operations is the production of talc, used for a variety of essential services. One-third of the talc produced in the United States comes from the mines of St. Lawrence County (6).

3

6

1

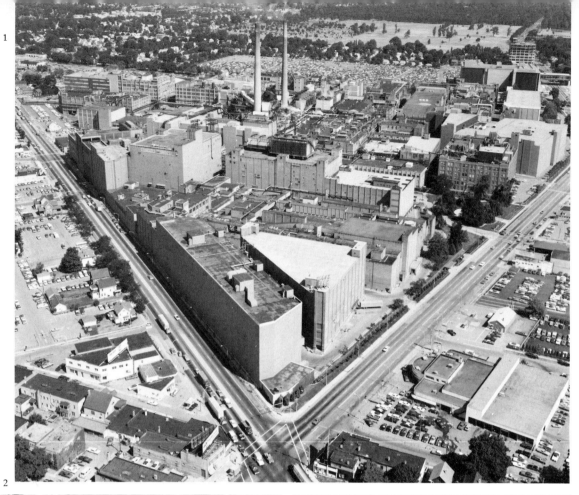

2

For almost a century the Eastman Kodak Company (1) has been intimately associated with the economy of the Rochester area. Boxes containing thousands of cylinders of film stored in Eastman warehouses suggest the gigantic scope of this enterprise (2). The Bausch & Lomb Optical Company, also in Rochester, has for a century past produced lenses of exceptional quality. Here a lens is being inspected (3). More than a dozen other Rochester companies make optical goods. Throughout the area, precision in manufacturing operations requires a highly skilled working force, which enjoys a high level of income. Opposite, Xerox employees (4) calibrate gauges used in manufacturing operations. Centered in Rochester, the Xerox Corporation has been for decades one of the nation's fastest-growing enterprises. At Corning, precision manufacturing was spectacularly demonstrated with the production of the world's largest telescopic lens, a two-hundred-inch disk, for the Mount Palomar Observatory (5).

OVERLEAF: For many of the leading industrial corporations of the state and nation, New York City remains the center of management. More than any other American city, New York provides complex facilities of finance, marketing, and communications, without which big business cannot effectively function.

# *Education*

Over the past century the educational facilities of New York State have been constantly strained to meet its inhabitants' mounting needs. The public elementary schools were long faced with the problem of opening the way for immigrant children, or the children of recent immigrants, to become literate and be indoctrinated with American values like these girls in a New York City classroom (1). Privately endowed institutions, such as Cooper Union in New York City, provided practical education and cultural programs without charge (2), as did the City University of New York with its four free colleges serving thousands of students. Also in the metropolis, Columbia University—the King's College of colonial days—had long since become an outstanding community of scholars (3), along with New York University and Fordham University. With Cornell University, whose College of Agriculture is shown here (4), New York State first developed a plan for contracting with private institutions to provide public instruction in various fields, a policy extended to other colleges with special educational programs. In 1948 the legislature created the State University of New York, which now has campuses across the state, including one at Albany, where the campus, incorporating its remarkable Carillon Tower (5), is a major architectural landmark. Union (6) and Colgate (7) are among the best known of the state's more than two hundred universities, colleges, and professional schools.

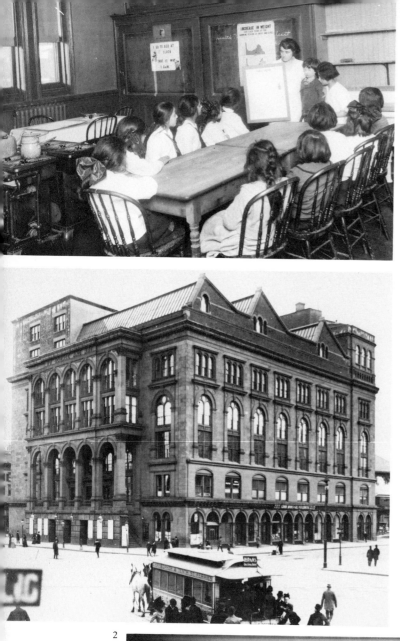

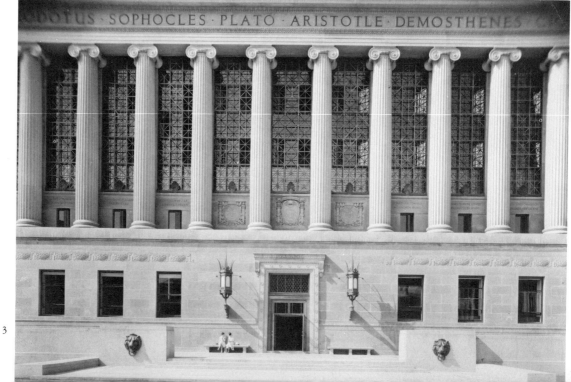

3

2

# A New Albany

During the night of March 28–29, 1911, a fire broke out in the Assembly library of the Capitol that threatened to destroy the entire "fireproof" building (1). Almost a half-million books and more than a quarter-million manuscripts, many of them of the utmost historic interest, were lost. However, the bulk of the structure escaped serious damage and was soon restored from smoke and water damage. The architects responsible for the Capitol had envisioned it surrounded by a spacious, well-kept landscape, which would have called for the demolition of the aging rowhouses that hemmed in the site. In 1962 Governor Nelson Rockefeller and the legislature, in cooperation with the city of Albany, set in motion the dramatic Empire State Plaza project, which would at last give the Capitol an ambience worthy of its importance. The next year, demolition of entire city blocks of decrepit surrounding structures was undertaken over an area of ninety-eight acres. Along that opened corridor a magnificent concourse, with an assemblage of modern governmental buildings lining an axis of pools and fountains, would stretch for a half mile south of the Capitol. At the southernmost extremity of this complex the Cultural Education Center, terminating the design, would look back toward the old Capitol at the other end of the Mall (2).

# *Ethnic Groups*

7

New York is a house of many mansions, each one teeming with life. At midcentury almost one-quarter of all foreign-born residents of the United States lived in the state—principally Italians, Russians (mostly Jewish), Poles, Germans, Irish, Austrians, and British. During and following World War I great waves of blacks from the South also settled in the state as more workers were needed. During World War II a tide of immigrants from Puerto Rico also arrived. Many New York cities bear witness to this phenomenal ethnic mixture, but it is most dramatically apparent in New York City, where there are about the same number of different national and racial groups as are represented in the United Nations. A rack of local ethnic newspapers, part of a bicentennial display at Rockefeller Plaza (1), testifies to the variety of local ethnic groups. Many of the groups, like the Chinese (2), Italians (3), and Puerto Ricans (4), still cluster in their own neighborhoods, where they have access to food and other goods of their homeland, and can more easily retain their language and customs. Many Orthodox Jews still dress distinctively (5) and continue to speak Yiddish. A midtown New York City street shows the variety of ethnic restaurants (6). A number of ethnic groups have annual parades on Fifth Avenue. One such parade, by Greek-Americans, is shown here (7).

# History

In New York State the past is present, as may be seen in the survival and restoration of innumerable historic monuments. A seventeenth-century house, with leaded glass windows, still stands at Cutchogue on Long Island (1), and at Newburgh the stone house which Washington used as his headquarters still survives (2). In the Champlain Valley, Fort Ticonderoga, which played such a pivotal role at various points in the French and Indian War and in the American Revolution, has been reconstructed to its earlier appearance (3). Johnson Hall (4), built in Johnstown shortly after the French and Indian War by Sir William Johnson, who was a significant figure in Anglo-Indian and American-Indian affairs over a period of decades, is now owned by the State of New York, together with a small stone building close to it that was one of two blockhouses built to protect the mansion from attack. Farther west, near Youngstown, Fort Niagara has been restored to look much as it did under three flags— French, British, and American (5)—more than two hundred years ago. At Cooperstown the New York State Historical Association has reassembled a wide variety of relics to show what upper New York State was like in times past; among them are the Farmer's Museum, an old-time drugstore, a printing office, a schoolhouse, and numerous examples of folk art (6).

4

5
6

309

## Natural Wonders

New York is a state rich in varied natural wonders and scenic beauties, from the lordly Hudson River, with its palisades and highlands, to the great cataracts of Niagara Falls. To protect those sites and sights and preserve them as recreational attractions, many of them have been brought within the almost eighty state-administered parks. The most spectacular natural feature of the state is Niagara Falls (1), which years ago, with the cooperation of Canada, was set apart as a sightseeing reservation—a departure in planning, new at the time, that was significant for park policy throughout the nation. On the west bank of the Hudson, miles of shoreline, including Storm King Mountain (2), have been set aside to form Palisades Interstate Park, which extends inland to cover vast tracts of land in Rockland and Orange counties. With a few hours' drive, most New Yorkers can reach the chasm cut deep in the rocks at Watkins Glen in the Finger Lakes district (3) or the Ausable River (4), which flows through another deep gorge as it tumbles down from the Adirondacks. As earlier told, much of the forested highlands of the Catskills (5) and the Adirondacks (6) have been set aside as a perpetual wilderness preserve, the largest protected area of the kind in the entire nation.

2

3

4

5

6

# Bibliography

ADAMS, JAMES TRUSLOW. *Album of American History,* vol. 1–6. New York, 1944.

ALBION, ROBERT GREENHALGH. *The Rise of New York Port.* New York, 1939.

ALBION, ROBERT GREENHALGH. *Square-Riggers on Schedule.* Princeton, 1938.

*The American Heritage Book of Great Historic Places.* New York, 1957.

*American Heritage Magazine.* New York, 1954–76.

*The American Heritage Pictorial Atlas of United States History.* New York, 1966.

ASBURY, HERBERT. *The Gangs of New York.* New York, 1928.

BARBER, JOHN WARNER. *Historical Collections of the State of New York.* New York, 1841.

BIDWELL, PERCY WELLS, and FALCONER, J. L. *History of Agriculture in the Northern United States.* Washington, D.C., 1925.

BISHOP, MORRIS. *Champlain, the Life of Fortitude.* New York, 1948.

BLIVEN, BRUCE. *Battle for Manhattan.* New York, 1956.

BROWN, RALPH H. *Mirror for Americans.* New York, 1943.

CARMAN, HARRY J., ed. *American Husbandry.* New York, 1939.

CARMER, CARL. *The Hudson.* New York, 1939.

CARMER, CARL. *Listen for a Lonesome Drum.* New York, 1950.

CARMER, CARL, ed. *The Tavern Lamps Are Burning.* New York, 1964.

CHRISTMAN, HENRY. *Tin Horns and Calico.* New York, 1945.

COLDEN, CADWALADER. *The History of the Five Indian Nations.* London, 1747.

DAVIDSON, MARSHALL B. *Life in America.* 2 vols. Boston, 1951.

DWIGHT, TIMOTHY. *Travels in New-England and New-York.* 4 vols. New Haven, 1821–22.

ELDRIDGE, PAUL. *Crown of Empire.* New York, 1957.

ELLIS, DAVID M., and others. *A History of New York State.* Ithaca, 1967.

EVERS, ALF. *The Catskills from Wilderness to Woodstock.* New York, 1972.

Federal Writers' Project. *New York: A Guide to the Empire State.* New York, 1940.

Federal Writers' Project. *New York City Guide.* New York, 1939.

Federal Writers' Project. *New York Panorama.* New York, 1938.

FOX, DIXON RYAN. *Yankees and Yorkers.* New York, 1940.

HANSEN, MARCUS LEE. *The Atlantic Migration.* Cambridge, 1940.

HOCHSCHILD, HAROLD K. *Township 34.* 7 vols. New York, 1952.

HOWAT, JOHN K. *The Hudson River and Its Painters.* New York, 1972.

JAMESON, JOHN FRANKLIN, ed. *Narratives of New Netherland.* New York, 1909.

KNIGHT, SARAH. *The Private Journal of a Journey from Boston to New York . . . 1704.* Albany, 1865.

KOUWENHOVEN, JOHN A. *The Columbia Historical Portrait of New York.* New York, 1953.

Life Library of America. *The Gateway States.* New York, 1967.

MACCRACKEN, HENRY NOBLE. *Old Dutchess Forever.* New York, 1956.

McMasters, John Bach. *A History of the People of the United States.* New York, 1883–1913.

Monaghan, Frank, and Lowenthal, Marvin. *This Was New York.* Garden City, 1943.

Morison, Samuel Eliot. *Samuel de Champlain.* Boston, 1972.

Nevins, Allan, ed. *Diary of Philip Hone.* New York, 1927.

Riis, Jacob A. *How the Other Half Lives.* New York, 1890.

Smith, Matthew Hale. *Sunshine and Shadow.* Hartford, 1868.

Stokes, I. N. Phelps, and Hood, Robert H. *The Iconography of Manhattan Island.* 6 vols. New York, 1915–1928.

Wainger, Bertrand M.; Furman, Dorothy W.; and Oagley, Edith Brooks. *Exploring New York.* 3rd ed. New York, 1956.

Wertenbaker, Thomas Jefferson. *The Founding of American Civilization: The Middle Colonies.* New York, 1938.

*Winslow Homer in the Adirondacks.* Blue Mountain Lakes, 1959.

# Picture Sources

Here is a list of abbreviations used in the picture credits:

AAS American Antiquarian Society, Worcester, Mass.
AIHA Albany Institute of History and Art
BM British Museum
CSS Charles Scribner's Sons Art Files
*Gleason's* *Gleason's Pictorial Drawing-Room Companion*
HABS Historic American Buildings Survey, Washington, D.C.
*HW* *Harper's Weekly*
LC Library of Congress, Washington, D.C.
*Leslie's* *Frank Leslie's Illustrated Newspaper*
MCNY Museum of the City of New York
MFA Museum of Fine Arts, Boston
MMA Metropolitan Museum of Art, New York
NA National Archives, Washington, D.C.
NGA National Gallery of Art, Washington, D.C.
NYCCC New York City Chamber of Commerce
NYHS New-York Historical Society
*NYIN* *New York Illustrated News*
NYPL New York Public Library
NYSDC New York State Department of Commerce
NYSHA New York State Historical Association
NYSL New York State Library
NYSM New York State Museum
SI Smithsonian Institution
*SM* *Scribner's Monthly*
*SMag* *Scribner's Magazine*

**x–xiii** S. Augustus Mitchell, *Mitchell's New General Atlas,* Phila., 1872. **18–19** 1,2. Champlain, *Voyages,* Paris, 1613. NYPL. 3. NYHS. 4. Adrian Block, *The First Figurative Map,* 1614. Copy, NYPL, Stokes Coll. **20–21** 1. BM. 2. Joost Hartgers, *Beschryvinghe. . . .* NYPL, Prints Div. 3. Museum of Science & Industry, N.Y. 4. Visscher, N., *Novi Belgii,* NYPL. 5. *Codex Canadansis,* c.1700. Thomas Gilcrease Inst. of American History & Art, Tulsa. 6. *A Moppe of Coll. Romer his journey . . . ,* 1700. Public Record Office, London. **22–23** 1. Joost Hartgers, *Beschryvinghe. . . .* NYPL, Prints Div. 2. De Manatus, *Op de Noort Rivier,* 1639. NYPL, Prints Div. 3. *Belgii Novi Angliae Novae . . . ,* c.1648. NPYL, Prints Div. 4. Edward Williams, *Virginia,* 1651. Va. State Library. 5. Father Louis Hennepin, *Nouvelle Decouverte . . . ,* 1697. **24–25** 1,4. NYHS. 2. Rijksmuseum, Amsterdam. 3. NYPL, Stokes Coll. 5. J. Milberti, *Itineraire Pittoresque du Fleuve Hudson,* 1828. NYHS. **26–27** 1. Sleepy Hollow Restorations, Tarrytown. 2. Philipsburg Manor. Coll., M. B. Davidson. 3,6. MMA. 4,5. Yale Univ. Art Gallery. **28–29** 1. AIHA. 2. MCNY. 3,4. MMA. 5. NYSHA. **30–31** 1. Greene County Hist. Soc., Coxsackie. 2. Hugue-

not Hist. Soc., New Paltz. 3,4. NYSDC. 5. Staten Island Hist. Soc. **32–33** 1,2,5. NYHS. 3,4. Private coll. **34–35** 1. Victoria & Albert Museum. 2. Hist. Soc. of the Tarrytowns. Photo: Frick Art Reference Library. 3. Mass. Art Commission. 4. NYHS. **36–37** 1–6. *A South Prospect of . . . New York,* c.1719. Coll., Edward W. C. Arnold. NYPL, Prints Div. **38–39** 1,3. Culver. 2. NYHS. 4. Hist. Soc. of Pa. **40–41** 1,5,6. LC. 2. NYHS. 3. Office of the Mayor, Albany. 4. BM. **42–43** 1,3. John Carter Brown Library. 2. AIHA. 4. CSS. 5. NYHS. 6. NYSHA. **44–45** 1. McCord Museum. 2. Coll., William H. Coverdale. 3. Fort Ticonderoga Museum. 4. Amherst College. 5. LC. **46–47** 1. NYHS. 2. NYPL. 3–5. Lent by Ethel M. Howell to MCNY. **48–49** 1. NYHS. 2. *Albany Gazette,* June 11, 1798. AIHA. 3. *Albany Gazette,* Dec. 6, 1798. AIHA. 4. *New York Mercury,* Jan. 7, 1765. 5. *New York Gazette* or *Weekly Post–Boy,* Aug. 16, 1764. 6. NYPL, Broadside Coll. **50–51** 1–3,5,6. MMA. 4. NYHS. **52–53** 1,3. Columbia Univ. 2. NYPL, Stokes Coll. 4. MMA. 5. NYPL, Prints Div. **54–55** 1. NYPL, Stokes Coll. 2. MCNY. 3,5. John Carter Brown Library. 4. NYHS. 6. LC. **56–57** 1. Washington and Lee Univ. 2,4. NYPL, Spencer Coll. 3. NA. 5. NYHS. 6. NYPL, Stokes Coll. **58–59** 1,5. NYPL, Stokes Coll. 2. NYPL, Emmet Coll. 3. NYPL, Manuscripts and Archives Div. 4. Fordham Univ. Photo: Frick Art Reference Library. **60–61** 1. Copyright: Frick Coll. 2. Manoir Richelieu Coll. 3,5. Public Archives of Canada. 4. Wadsworth Atheneum. **62–63** 1. NYPL, Manuscripts and Archives Div. 2. T. K. Anburey, *Travels Through America,* 1789. NYPL. 3. MMA. 4. Independence Nat'l Historical Park Coll. 5. NYPL, Prints Div. **64–65** 1. LC. 2. NYPL, Emmet Coll. 3. Anne S. K. Brown Military Coll., Brown Univ. Library. 4. MMA. 5. Yale Univ. Art Gallery. 6. Recut from Francis Bailey, *Continental Almanac,* 1781. **66–67** 1. NYPL, Stokes Coll. 2. NGA, Mellon Coll. 3. John Carter Brown Library. 4. NA. 5. MMA. 6. Independence Hall. **68–69** 1. NYCCC. 2. NGA. 3–5. NYHS. **70–71** 1,4. NYPL, Stokes Coll. 2. NYHS. 3. LC. **72–73** 1,2. Hist. Soc. of Pa. 3. MMA. 4,5. NYHS. **74–75** 1. NYHS. 2. NYPL. 3,4. MCNY. **76–77** 1–5,7,8. MCNY, Edward W. C. Arnold Coll. 6. MMA, Edward W. C. Arnold Coll. **78–79** 1,3. MMA. 2. NYHS. 4,5. DuPont Winterthur Museum. 6. NYPL. **80–81** 1. Boscobel Restoration. 2. Delaware County Hist. Assoc. 3. HABS, LC. 4. Foundation Hist. Assoc., Auburn. 5,6. NYSHA. **82–83** 1. Peale Museum, Baltimore. 2. NYHS. 3. NYPL, Stokes Coll. 4,5. MCNY. **84–85** 1. NYHS. 2. Henry S. Cooper family. 3. Clark Estates, Inc. Photo: NYSHA. 4. NYPL, Stokes Coll. 5. Jefferson County Hist. Soc. **86–87** 1. *The*

*Port Folio,* Aug. 1815. 2. William Clements Library, Univ. of Michigan. 3. NYPL, Emmett Coll. 4. Art Commission of the City of N.Y. 5. NYPL, Stokes Coll. 6. NYHS. **88–89** 1. *New York Magazine,* or *Literary Repository,* Mar. 1791. NYHS. 2. West Point Museum Coll. 3. *Analectic Magazine,* July–Dec. 1820. 4. Yale Univ. Art Gallery. **90–91** 1,4. NYSHA. 2. Cadwallader D. Colden, *Memoir Prepared for the Celebration of the Completion of the New York Canals,* 1825. 3. NYHS. 5. MCNY. **92–93** 1. NYHS. **94–95** 1,2. NYHS. 3–5. NYPL, Stokes Coll. **96–97** 1. NYPL, Stokes Coll. 2. MMA. 3. NYHS. 4. Coll., Seaman's Bank for Savings. 5. NYSHA. **98–99** 1,6. NYSHA. 2,5. NYHS. 3,4,7. MMA. **100–101** 1–4. CSS. 5. Kennedy Galleries. **102–103** 1. CSS. **104–105** 1,6. MMA. 2. New Britain Museum of American Art. 3. AIHA. 4. MFA. 5. NYSHA. **106–107** 1. Museums at Stony Brook. 2,3. MMA. 4. NYSHA. 5. Century Assoc. **108–109** 1. Sleepy Hollow Restorations, Tarrytown. 2. Yale Univ. Art Gallery. 3. NGA, Mellon Coll. 4,6. NYPL. 5. Coll. Nat'l. Academy of Design. Photo: Frick Art Reference Library. **110–111** 1. NYPL, Stokes Coll. 2,3. NYHS. 4. NYPL. 5. MMA. 6. Lyndhurst Nat'l. Trust for Historic Preservation. **112–113** 1–7. MCNY, Coll., Mrs. Luke Vincent Lockwood. **114–115** 1. MCNY. 2. Ex-Coll., Mrs. Luke Vincent Lockwood. 3–5. *NYIN,* Feb. 11, 1860. MCNY. 6. *Leslie's,* Aug. 13, 1859. **116–117** 1,4. NYHS. 2,3. NYPL, Stokes Coll. **118–119** 1. NYPL, Stokes Coll. 2. NYPL, Eno Coll. 3,5. MCNY. 4. LC. **120–121** 1,2,5. MCNY. 3. *Leslie's,* Feb. 26, 1859. 4. MFA. Photo: Newark Museum. **122–123** 1. CSS. 2. Cornell Univ. 3. Old Print Shop. 4. NYHS. 5. LC. **124–125** 1,2,4,5. NYHS. 3. MCNY. **126–127** 1. NYPL. 2. LC. 3. NYPL, Prints Div. 4. Property of Col. J. M. Sherwood, Auburn. 5. *Leslie's,* July 25, 1857. 6. Coll., M. B. Davidson. **128–129** 1. NYSHA. 2. David Murray, *Delaware County, New York: History of the Century,* 1898. 3. Historic Cherry Hill, Albany. 4. NYSL. **130–131** 1. NYPL, Rare Book Div. 2,3. NYPL. 4. *Leslie's,* Mar. 12, 1859. NYPL. 5. *Albany Argus,* Oct. 20, 1846. NYHS. 6. *Buffalo Republican,* Nov. 2, 1833. NYHS. **132–133** 1,2 *Annual Pictorial Herald,* Jan. 1, 1846. 3. Albright–Knox Art Gallery, Buffalo. 4. Hudson River Museum, Yonkers. 5. MCNY. 6. Museums at Stony Brook. **134–135** 1,2,4. MCNY. 3. NYPL, Prints Div. 5. *American Magazine,* vol. 2, 1835. 6. Old Print Shop. **136–137** 1,2. Union College Library. 3. Hamilton College. 4. Colgate Univ. Library. 5. NYHS. 6. MCNY. **138–139** 1. NYHS. 2. NYSHA. 3,6. MCNY. 4,5. Jockey Club. **140–141** 1. *NYIN,* Aug. 4, 1860. NYPL. 2. NYPL, Manuscripts and Archives Div. 3. *Leslie's,* 1866. NYPL. 4. St. Louis Art Museum. 5. NYPL. 6. MFA. **142–143** 1. LC. 2. Minneapolis Inst. of Arts. 3. Old Print Shop. 4. MFA. **144–145** 1,3. NYPL. 2,4,6. MCNY. 5. LC. **146–147** 1,2. MCNY. 3. NYHS. 4. LC. 5. NA. **148–149** 1,3. *Harper's Magazine,* Nov. 1854. 2. MFA. 4,6. MCNY. 5. *Leslie's,* May 15, 1875. NYPL. **150–151** 1. Brigham Young Univ., Provo, Utah. 2. Fruitlands Museums. 3. AAS. 4. *HW,* 1859. LC. 5. NYPL, Picture Coll. 6. *NYIN,* Oct. 29, 1853. **152–153** 1. NYSM. 2,3. Oneida Ltd. Silversmiths, Oneida. 4. *HW,* Sept. 10, 1859. **154–155** 1,3. *NYIN,* July 16, 1853. 2,4. *NYIN,* Sept. 3, 1853. **156–157** 1. NYPL, Eno Coll. 2,6. MCNY. 3. Otis Elevator Co., N.Y. 4. *HW,* Oct. 16, 1858. NYPL. 5. *Gleason's,* Nov 11, 1854. **158–159** 1. NYSHA. 2–4. NYPL, Stokes Coll. 5. NYHS. **160–161** 1,2. NYPL, Stokes Coll. **162–163** 1. *New York Herald,* Apr. 15, 1861. 2. MFA. 3. CSS. 4. West Point Museum Coll. 5. MCNY. 6. Anne S. K. Brown Military Coll., Brown Univ. Library. **164–165** 1. *HW,* Dec. 28, 1861. MCNY. 2. *Valentine's Manual,* 1864. NYPL. 3. *Leslie's,* Nov. 7, 1863. NYPL. 4,5. *HW,* Nov. 7, 1863. Newark Public Library. **166–167** 1. *Leslie's,* Mar. 19, 1864. NYPL. 2. *Illustrated London News,* Apr. 8, 1865. 3,5. *Illustrated London News,* Aug. 15, 1863. 4. *HW,* Aug. 1, 1863. 6. *Illustrated London News,* Aug. 8 1863. **168–169** 1. MCNY. 2. MMA. 3. Putnam County Hist. Soc., Cold Spring. 4. NYHS. **170–171** 1. MCNY. 2. Photo: Mathew Brady. 3. *Leslie's,* Oct. 16, 1869. 4. After a photo by Mathew Brady. 5. NYPL, Prints Div. **172–173** 1. Otis Elevator Co., N.Y. 2. *Leslie's,* 1873. LC. 3. Bausch & Lomb Optical Co. 4. Corning Glass Works. 5,6. CSS. **174–175** 1–5. *Asher & Adams' Pictorial Album of American Industry,* 1876. **176–177** 1. AAS. 2. United Shoe Machinery Co., Boston. 3. CSS. 4. Coll., Carl Dreppard. 5. *Leslie's,* Aug. 22, 1857. 6. NYHS. **178–179** 1. *American Artisan,* Feb. 1, 1871. 2,4,5. Arthur J. Weise, *The City of Troy & Its Vicinity,* 1886. 3. SI. **180–181** 1. MFA, Springfield. 2. MFA. 3. NYSHA. 4. MMA. 5. Museum of Art, Rhode Island School of Design. **182–183** 1. NYSHA. **184–185** 1,2. *Leslie's,* Dec. 21, 1878. 3. *Harper's Monthly,* Nov. 1875. 4,5. NYPL, Picture Coll. 6. *HW,* Jan. 31, 1885. NYPL, Picture Coll. **186–187** 1,5. *History of Seneca County,* Phila.: Everts, Ensign & Everts, 1876. 2,3. F. W. Beers, *County Atlas of Orange,* Chicago: Andreas, Baskin & Burr, 1875. 4,6. *Combination Atlas Map of Genesee County,* Phila.: Everts, Ensign & Everts, 1876. **188–189** 1–7. *Combination Atlas Map of Genesee County,* Phila., Everts, Ensign & Everts, 1876. **190–191** 1. LC. **192–193** 1–3. NYPL, Picture Coll. 4,5. CSS. **194–195** 1–5. NYSL. **196–197** 1–11. NYSL. **198–199** 1. MFA. 2. LC. 3–5. NYPL, Picture Coll. **200–201** 1. N.Y. Board of Transportation. 2. *Leslie's,* Sept. 7, 1878. NYPL. 3. *HW,* Feb. 9, 1878. 4. *Leslie's,* Nov. 15, 1879. 5. *The Daily Graphic,* May 8, 1878. NYPL. 6. James D. McCabe, Jr., *New York By Sunlight & Gaslight,* 1882. NYPL. 7. *Leslie's,* Nov. 1, 1879. Newark Public Library. **202–203** 1. MCNY. 2. *Harper's New Monthly Magazine,* May 1883. Newark Public Library. 3. *HW.* 4. *Leslie's,* May 26, 1883. Newark Public Library. 5. *HW,* May 26, 1883. **204–205** 1,2. *HW,* Oct. 29, 1887. 3,4. *HW,* Dec. 14, 1889. 5. N.Y.C. Bureau of Water Supply. **206–207** 1. Biltmore House & Gardens, Biltmore Estate. 2–5. MCNY. **208–209** 1. NYPL. 2. *Gleason's,* Feb. 25, 1854. NYPL. 3. *HW,* Nov. 6, 1880. 4. *SM,* Aug. 1871. 5. *Leslie's,* Mar. 9, 1872. 6. *Leslie's,* June 7, 1873. NYPL. **210–211** 1. NYHS. 2. LC. 3. MCNY. 4. *HW,* Nov. 6, 1886. NYPL, Picture Coll. **212–213** 1. NYHS. 2. MMA. 3,4. MCNY. 5–7. *HW,* Jan. 21, 1882. **214–215** 1. James D. McCabe, Jr., *Lights & Shadows of New York Life,* 1872. 2–4. *The Daily Graphic,* Aug. 26, 1879. NYPL. 5. *Leslie's,* Sept. 7, 1889. 6. Robert DeForest, *Tenement House Problem,* 1903. 7. James Gallatin, *Tenement House Reform in the City of N.Y.,* 1881. **216–217** 1–3. CSS. 4. *HW,* Aug. 3, 1867. 5. Corcoran Gallery. 6. *Leslie's,* 1881. LC. **218–219** 1. *HW,* Feb. 29, 1896. 2. CSS. 3,4. LC. Photo: J. A. Riis. 5. Nat'l. Park Service. **220–221** 1,6. *SM,* Apr. 1881. 2. MCNY. 3. Plumbing & Heating Industries Bureau, Chicago. 4. Frederick Opper, 1883. 5. *HW,* May 2, 1874. **222–223** 1,2. MCNY. 3. *HW,* Apr. 25, 1903. 4. *Harper's Bazaar,* Dec. 7, 1895. 5. *HW,* Nov. 21, 1896. 6. Art Inst. of Chicago. 7. Corcoran Gallery. **224–225** 1. James D. McCabe, Jr., *Lights & Shadows of New York Life,* 1872. 2. *Hearth & Home,* May 6, 1871. 3. *Hearth & Home,* Apr. 22, 1871. 4. *Hearth & Home,* June 26, 1869. 5. CSS. **226–227** 1. LC. 2. *Leslie's,* July 26, 1890. 3. *SMag,* July 1892. 4. *HW,*

Apr. 26, 1890. 5. Photo: ILGWU. **228–229** 1. *HW*, Aug. 4, 1877. 2. *Leslie's*, Aug. 16, 1873. 3. *HW*, Sept. 14, 1872. 4. Photo: Ruth H. Smiley. 5. CSS. 6. NYPL, Picture Coll. **230–231** 1. MCNY. **232–233** 1,2. LC. 3. Piping Rock Country Club, Locust Valley. 4. U.S. Golf Assoc. 5. MCNY. **234–235** 1. *The Daily Graphic,* June 16, 1877. NYPL. 2. *HW*, Oct. 13, 1883. NYPL. 3. *Leslie's*, Dec. 9, 1882. 4. NYPL. 5. LC. **236–237** 1. *SM*, Aug. 1871. 2. Vassar College Library. 3. *Leslie's*, July 10, 1875. 4. *SM*, June 1873. 5. Cornell Univ., Dept. of Manuscripts & Univ. Archives. 6. NA. **238–239** 1. *HW*, Aug. 21, 1881. **240–241** 1. *Dictionary of American Portraits*, Dover Publications, 1967. 2,7. Olana State Historic Site, Taconic State Park & Recreation Commission. 3–6. HABS, Photos: Cervin Robinson. **242–243** 1. F.O.C. Darley, from Washington Irving, *The Sketch Books of Geoffrey Crayon*, 1848. NYPL, Prints Div. 2. SI. 3. *Leslie's*, Jan. 11, 1890. 4,5. LC. 6. NYPL, Picture Coll. **244–245** 1. Concord Free Library. 2. North Woods Club. Photo: Adirondack Museum. 3. NGA. 4. Phila. Museum of Art. 5. Worcester Art Museum. 6. Henry Gallery, Univ. of Wash. **246–247** 1–6. Adirondack Museum, Blue Mountain Lake. **248–249** 1,2,5. AT&T. 3. NYHS. 4. *Leslie's*, Jan. 29, 1887. **250–251** 1,2. *The Daily Graphic,* Dec. 22, 1880. 3. *SM*, July 1880. 4. LC. 5. Edison Nat'l. Historic Site, Nat'l. Park Service. 6. *HW*, June 24, 1882. 7. Con Ed. **252–253** 1,3. G.E. 2. *The Electrical World,* Aug. 25, 1888. 4. *The Electrical World,* Apr. 14, 1888. 5. MCNY. 6. Corning Museum. **254–255** 1. Corcoran Gallery. 2. *Scientific American*, Oct. 20, 1894. 3. *Scientific American*, Mar. 5, 1892. 4. *Scientific American*, Apr. 4, 1896. **256–257** 1,3,4. Coll., Stephen D. Maguire. 2. NYSHA, Smith–Telfer Coll. 5. MCNY. **258–259** 1–5. NYSHA, Smith–Telfer Coll. **260–261** 1. LC. 2,4,5. NYSHA, Smith–Telfer Coll. 3. Int'l. Museum of Photography, George Eastman House. **262–263** 1. NYHS. 2. Pa. Academy of the Fine Arts. 3. Fogg Art Museum. 4,8. NYPL. 5,7. CSS. 6. Frick Art Reference Library. 9. Photo: John D. MacDonald. **264–265** 1,2,4. MCNY. 3,5. LC. 6. Woolworth. **266–267** 1,5,6. MCNY. 2. NYHS. 3. James D. McCabe, Jr., *Lights & Shadows of New York Life*, 1872. 4. Penn Central Co. **268–269** 1–3. MCNY. 4,5. LC. 6. U.S. Army Signal Corps. 7. Hempstead Library. **270–271** 1. NYHS. 2,5. Brown Brothers. 3. LC. 4. Morgan Guaranty Trust Co. **272–273** 1. Detroit Inst. of Arts. 2. MMA. 3. Yale Univ. Art Gallery. 4. *HW*, Feb. 17, 1900. 5. L.A. County Museum of Art. 6. Cleveland Museum of Art. **274–275** 1. NYHS. 2. U.S. Army Signal Corps. 3. Red Cross. 4. CSS. 5. Committee on Public Info., Wash., D.C. 6. Int'l. News. **276–277** 1,2. MCNY. 3. NYPL, Prints Div. 4. LC. 5. NYHS. 6. Brown Brothers.. **278–279** 1. NYHS. 2. Coll., Jean Lipman. 3. NYPL, Picture Coll. 4. *The New Yorker Magazine,* Inc. 5. Babe Ruth Foundation. 6. Culver Pictures. 7. N.Y. *Times*, Oct. 1929. **280–281** 1. Brown Brothers. 2–5. Farm Security Admin. 6. Rockefeller Center. **282–283** 1. NYPL, Picture Coll. 2. NA. 3. Wide World. 4. N.Y. World's Fair Publicity Dept. **284–285** 1,3. Wide World. 2. UPI. 4. Curtiss–Wright Corp. 5. Assoc. of American Railroads. **286–287** 1. U.S. Bureau of Printing & Engraving. 2. LC. 3. CSS. 4–8. Wide World. **288–289** 1. Fairchild Aerial Surveys, Inc. 2,3. NYSDC. 4. Port of N.Y. Authority. 5. U.S. Steel Corp. 6. Triborough Bridge & Tunnel Authority. **290–291** 1. Pan Am. 2. American Airlines. 3,4. Port Authority of N.Y. & N.J. 5. Allegheny. **292–293** 1,2,4,5. NYSDC. 3. St. Lawrence Seaway Development Corp. **294–295** 1–4. NYSDC. **296–297** 1. G.E. 2. Alco Engines Division, White Motor Corp. 3,4. Bethlehem Steel. 5. IBM. 6. Gouverneur Talc Co. **298–299** 1,2. Kodak. 3. Bausch & Lomb. 4. Xerox. 5. Corning Glass Works. **300–301** 1. NYSDC. **302–303** 1. CSS. 2. Cooper Union. 3. Columbia Univ. 4. Cornell Univ. 5–7. NYSDC. **304–305** 1. AIHA. 2. Empire State Plaza Public Info. Office. **306–307** 1,6. Photos: Norman Kotkcr. 2,3,5. Photos: C. S. Varon. 4. P.A.L. 7. Greek Orthodox Archdiocese. **308–309** 1–6. NYSDC. **310–311** 1–6. NYSDC.

# *Index*

The index of this book serves as a guide to both textual and pictorial material. The contents of the pictures themselves are indexed in a great many cases, as explained in the introductory note, *This Book and Its Uses,* on page vii. The following system of reference is used:

187     reference to the text only or to both text and pictures on page 187

187:6     not mentioned in the text but depicted in picture number 6 on page 187

187:**6**     depicted in picture number 6 on page 187 and mentioned in the accompanying text

The number preceding the colon is the page number; the number following the colon is the picture number. When the identification of a subject is not obvious, an explanation of its position appears in parentheses following the page and picture number: e.g. architecture, Romanesque Revival, 193:5 (at right). When it seems desirable, dates are given to place a subject in its proper time frame.

East River (*continued*)
  views of:
      c.1717, 36–37
      1776, 54:**1**
      c.1836, 168:**1** (foreground)
      c.1974, 300–301 (at right)
Eastman, George, 13
  camera of, 173:**6**
  factory of, 173:**5**
Eastman Kodak Company, factory at Rochester,
      173:**5**, 298:**1,2**
economy, *see also* business and finance; industry;
      manufacturing; trade
      19c., 8, 12, 144–45
      20c., 13, 14, 270–71, 280–81
Edison, Thomas Alva:
  incandescent bulb designed by, 251:**5**
  machine works, 252–53:**1,3**, 252:**2**
Edison Electric Light Company, lighting station,
      1882, 251:**7**
Edouart, Augustin, silhouette by, 110:**3**
education, 52–53, 88–89, 134–37, 175:**5**, 191,
      219:**4**, 236–39, 302–03; *see also* colleges
      and universities; schools
Edward, Fort, plan of, 42:**1** (bottom)
"Eight," the, 272–73
Eisenhower, Dwight D., 293:**3** (right center)
Eisenhower, Mamie, 293:3 (at right)
Eisenhower Lock, St. Lawrence Seaway, 293:**4**
Elba, New York, factory in, 187:**6**
electric light, *see* electrification
electric power plant, 292:1 (at left)
electrification:
      bank, Cooperstown, 261:**4**
      Brush Electrical Station, 252:**4**
      of city streets, 250:**1,2,4**, 251:**6,7**
      at Coney Island, 250–51:**3**
      Edison machine works, 252–53:**1,3**, 252:**2**
      incandescent bulb, 251:**5**, 253:**6**
      power from Niagara Falls, 255
      Tiffany lamp, 253:**5**
      of transportation, 200, 256–57
elephants, in amusement park, 230–31 (center)
elevated railroads:
      in operation, 19c., 200–201
      planned, 1848, 117:**3**
      station at Sixth Ave. and 23rd St., New York City,
        201:**6**
elevators:
      in apartment houses, 220
      exhibit of, at 1853 World's Fair, 157:**3**
      grain, 158:**1** (left center), 192–93:**2** (left center),
        3, 193:**4**, 292:**2**
      at Lord and Taylor's store, 1873, 172:**2**
      Otis factory, 172:**1**, 198
      at railway stations, 117
Elgin Botanic Garden, New York City, 82–83:**3**
Elizabeth II, queen of England, 293:**3** (at left)
Ellis Island, immigration offices on, 217, 219:**5**
Elmira, New York, double-decker trolley at, 257:**4**
"Elysian Fields," Hoboken, New Jersey, 139:**3**
Emerson, Ralph Waldo, 7, 10, 245
Empire Springs, Saratoga, 142–43:**1** (at right)

"Empire" state, 7, 9, 12, 16
Empire State Building, New York City:
  completion of, 1931, 281:**5**
  view from, c.1974, 300–301
  view of, 1940s, 284–85:**5** (right center)
Empire State Plaza project, Albany, 304–05:**2**
Endicott, New York, 14, 296
England and English:
  colonial rule, 5–6, 36–39, 55
  in French and Indian War, 6, 42:**1,2,3**,
        43:**4,5**, 44–45
  immigration, 146:**1**, 217, 307
  Indian allies of, 40:3, 41:**4,5,6**, 43
  in Revolutionary War, 7, 54–67
  takeover from Dutch, 4, 5, 32, 34–35
  trade with, 11, 41
  in War of 1812, 8, 86–87
entertainments and amusements, *see also* fairs;
        parties; Saratoga; sports
  boating, 258:**2**
  circus, 180:**4**
  at Coney Island, 228:**1**, 230–31
  croquet, 259:**4**
  dancing, 120–21:**3**, 164–65:**5**, 115:**4**
  at "Elysian Fields," Hoboken, N.J., 139:**3**
  gambling, 50:**3**
  jumping rope, 258:**1**
  picnics, 34–35:**2**, 84:**1**
  reception, 1840, 110:**3**
  theater, 119:**5**, 138:**1,2**
  vacations, 142–43, 228:**2,3**, 229:**4**
Erie Canal, 10, 13, 14, 160
  at Buffalo, 1852, 158:**3** (lower left)
  cities along, 94–95
  extension, at Oswego, 158:**1**
  extension, at Troy, 1881, 190–91 (at right,
        parallel to Hudson)
  at Lockport, 1836, 96:**1**
  at Rochester, 1853, 158:**2** (foreground)
  trade on, 8, 11, 91:**3**, 92–93
  view of, 1830s, 92–93
Erie, Lake, 4, 8, 12, 123
  at Buffalo, 158:**3** (at left), 192–93:**2**
  industry on, 296:**3**, 297:**4**
  map of, 1771, 67:**4**
  steamboats on, 125:**5**
  views of:
      1813, 86:**1**
      1836, 94–95:**4**
Estonians, newspaper for (*Vaba Eesti Sona*), 306:**1**
ethnic groups, in 20c. New York City, 306–07;
        *see also* immigration
excavations:
  for Erie Canal, c.1820, 90:**2**
  for mastodon skeleton, 1801, 82:**1**
exhibits, at World's Fair, 1853, 156:**2**, 157:**3**
exploration, early, 4, 5, 18–19, 20:**1,2**
*Exhuming the First American Mastodon,* by
        C. W. Peale, 82:**1**
eyeglasses:
      c.1840, 150:**2**
      c.1900, 277:**4**
      store selling, 172:**3**

medicine (*continued*)
    insane asylum, Utica, 160–61:**2**
    at New York Hospital, 18c., 83:**4,5**
medicine cabinet, 188–89:**4**
meetinghouses, *see* churches
megaphone, 274:**4**
Melville, Herman, portrait of, 262:**3**
memorials, *see* monuments
Mencken, H. L., on Whitman, 262
merchandising, 48–49, *see also* stores; trade:
    18c., advertising
    of Singer sewing machine, 1901, 177:**6**
    vendors, New York City, 1840, 112–13
merchants, *see* occupations
Methodists, 46–47:**3**, 47:**5**
metrology laboratory, 299:**4**
Metropolitan Museum of Art, New York City:
    design for entrance to, 209:**4**
    opening reception of, 1872, 209:**5**
    Rensselaerwyck room, c.1765, 50–51:**1**
Metropolitan Opera House, New York City, 268:**1**
Middletown, New York, Orange County Press in, 186:**3**
*Middletown Daily Evening Press, see* newspapers
Milbourne, C., watercolor by, 74:**1**
milk, *see* dairy industry
milk can, 284:**3** (at top)
military, *see also* battles; navy; uniforms, military:
    British soldiers, 1755, 42:**1,3**
    camp, 1777, 62–63:**2**
    in Civil War, 11, 162–63
    in French and Indian War, 42:**1,3**
    in hospital, 1864, 164:**2**
    militia:
        and anti-rent riots, 1839, 128–29:**3**
        in Civil War, 1861, 162:**1**
        and draft riots, New York City, 1863, 167
        in War of 1812, 8
    parades of, New York City:
        1861, 162–63:**2**
        c.1917, 274–75:**2**
    recruitment:
        Civil War, 162:**1,3**, 163:**6**
        handbill, 1776, 55:**5**
        World War I, 274:**1**
    in Revolutionary War, 55:**5,6**, 58–67
    Russian sailors, 1863, 165:**4**
    supplies:
        Civil War, 168–69, 178
        World War I, 275:**5**
        World War II, 284–85:**4,5**
    transport:
        1755, 42:**3**
        1813, 86:**1**
        c.1917, 274:**3**
        c.1940, 284:**2**
    in War of 1812, 8, 86–87:**5**
    West Point Academy, 88–89
    World War II soldiers, 284:**2**
Millay, Edna St. Vincent, photograph of, 278:**3**
Miller, William, 10–11, 150:**2**
mills, *see also* factories:
    grain, c.1876, 186–87:**4**

    paper, 14
    at Rochester, New York, 13, 94:**2**, 127, 187
    water-powered, 18c., 34–35:**2** (at right)
Milne, A., watercolor by, 180:**1**
Mineola, Long Island, aircraft plant in, 1918, 275:**5**
Minerva, New York, view of farm near, 244–45:**2**
mining, 297:**6**
*Minnehaha* (steamboat), 143:**4**
Minuit, Peter, 22
mirrors:
    c.1860, 157:**5**
    bar, 1854, 141:**6**
Mitchell, Maria, 237
moccasins, 41:**5,6**
Mohawk and Hudson railroad, 9, 122:**1**
Mohawk Indians, 4
    costume:
        1710, 41:**5,6**
        18c., 43:**6**
    in French and Indian War, 43:**5**
    language, 43
    in Revolutionary War, 66–67:**1**, 66:**2**
    trip to London, 1709–10, 40:**3**, 41:**4,5,6**
Mohawk River:
    at Utica, 160
    views of:
        in 1780, 66–67:**1**
        18c., 43:**4** (marked Q)
        at Falls of Cohoes, 100–101:**2**
        near Randall, 293:**5**
Mohawk River Valley, 3, 6, 61, 66–67
Mohonk, Lake, hotel on, 229:**4**
Monroe County Court House, Rochester, New York, 158:**2** (large white building with cupola, at center)
Montcalm, 4
Montgomery County, view in, 293:**5**
monuments:
    historic, 308–09
    Soldiers' and Sailors' Monument, Buffalo, 193:**5**
    to Col. F. D. Wood, at West Point, 88–89:**4** (at right)
moose, skeleton of, displayed, 209:**6**
Morgan, J. P.:
    and Panic of 1907, 271:**5**
    portrait of, 271:**4**
Morgan, James Spencer, 10
Mormons, 10, 150:**1**
Moroni, Angel, presenting Book of Mormon to Joseph Smith, 150:**1**
Morrill Land-Grant Act, of 1862, land scrip issued under, 237:**6**
Morris, George P., residence of, 100–101:**3**
Morris, Gouverneur, 39
Morris, Lewis, yacht of, 51:**5**
Morris, Robert, 7
Morris, Roger, home of, 80:**3**
Morrisania manor, 51
Morse, Samuel F. B., 80
    portrait of William Cullen Bryant by, 109:**5**
    telegraph, 137
    *View from Apple Hill* by, 85:**3**
Morton, Gen. Jacob, bowl presented by, 72:**3**

occupations:
    actor, 138:**1,2**
    aircraft assembly worker, 275:5, 284–85:4
    artisan, 69:**4**
    artist, 105:**5**
    baker, 76:**5**
    banker, 145:**6**, 261:**4**
    barber, 55:**6**
    bartender, 141:6, 260:3, 272:1
    baseball player, 140–41:1
    blacksmith, 79:6 (left center)
    bootblack, 148–49:**2**
    bridge builder, 202:3
    butcher, 112:**2**
    caddy, 232–33:4
    canal boatman, 91:3, 92–93
    carpenter, 34, 49:6, 78:2
    clock and watch maker, 48
    construction worker, 49:6, 79:6 (lower right),
        90:2, 91:3 (at right), 204:1, 204–05:2,
        256–57:2, 289:4
    dairy farmer, 184–85:**1**, 294:2
    doctor, 164:2 (at right)
    dog killer, 76:**3**
    electrical worker, 251:6,7
    factory worker, 176–77:4
    farmer, 5, 7–8, 10, 13–14, 28:**5**, 66, 79:6
        (lower left), 106–07, 126:**3,5**, 184–85:**1**,
        197:11, 294:2
    ferryman, 27, 37:**5**
    fireman, 46–47:**2**, 76–77:**2**, 119:**5**, 157:4,
        163:**5**, 201:**4**, 282–83:2
    fruit vendor, 306:2
    garbage man, 77:**8**
    garment worker, 214:4, 226–27
    health inspector, 214:4, 217:**6**
    hospital attendant, 164:2 (at left)
    ironworker, 49:**5**, 168:2, 169:3
    jockey, 139:6
    judge, 180–81:5 (at right)
    lamplighter, 120:**1,2**
    locomotive engineer, 186–87:2, 200:2
    logger, 14, 245:5
    longshoreman, 96:1
    machine operator, 174:2, 252:2
    mechanic, 5, 79:6 (right center)
    merchant, 5, 19, 48, 72, 112–13, 145:5
    newsboy, 132:**3**, 132–33:**4**, 145:6, 186:3
    night watchman, 76:1
    omnibus driver, 116:1, 117:4
    pawnbroker, 144:4
    peddler, 76–77:**6**
    pewterer, 69:**4**
    photographer, 159:5 (lower right)
    plumber, 119:**4**
    police:
        c.1800, 77
        1859, 115:6
        1895, 235:5
        1934, 283:4
    porter, 75:**4**
    preacher, 152–53:4
    pressmen, 130:2

    ragpicker, 214:**3**
    railroad conductor, 242:4
    railroad construction worker, 256–57:2
    sailor, 5, 217:6
    sandwich board advertising men, 248–49:3
    sculptor, 210–11:**2**
    seamstress, 176:3, 177:6
    sewing machine operator, 214:4
    shipwright, 96–97:**5**
    silversmith, 27
    soldiers, 56, 162–63:2, 163:6
    stockbroker, 72, 170–71:3
    storekeeper, 307:5
    tanner, 242:3
    teacher, 134:**2**, 135:**6**, 302:1
    telephone operator, 248:**1**, 248–49:**2**
    telephone worker, 249:4
    vendor, 112–13
    vendor, street, 112:1, 218–19:2
    water seller, 77:**7**
    waiter, 222:1, 5, 272:1
    waitress, 222–23:2
    winemaker, 185:4,5
O'Connell, Daniel, bust of, 149:6 (at center)
oil, lamp, whales slaughtered for, 185:6
oil storage tanks, 292:1 (at right)
Olana, 240–41
Old Fly Market, New York City, view of, c.1810, 76–
    77:4
Olmstead, Frederick Law, portrait of, 206:1
Omnibuses, 116:1, 117:4, 144:3 (at right), 145:6,
    156–57:1 (left foreground), 248–49:3
Oneida Community, 152:2, 153:3
Oneida County, New York:
    apple growing, 14
    cheese manufacture, 184
Oneida Indians, 4
Oneonta, Cooperstown and Richfield Springs Railway,
    construction of, 256–57:2
onions, 8, 13
Onondaga Indians, 4
Onondaga Lake, at Syracuse, 1850, 160–61:1
Ontario, Fort, 87, 158:1 (at far left, foreground)
Ontario, Lake, 13
    map of, 1771, 67:4
    map of, 1871, x–xi
    views of:
        1804, 86:2 (left)
        1950, 158:1 (foreground)
opera houses:
    at Batavia, 1876, 188:2
    in New York City, 268:1
opium pipe, 218:1 (at right)
optical instruments, 13, 172:3, 299:**3,5**
Orange, Fort, 5, *see also* Albany
Orange County:
    Palisades Interstate Park, 310:2
    view of Warwick, c.1875, 186–87:2
Orange County Press, Middletown, New York, 186:3
orchard, apple, 295:3
orchestra, theater, 1822, 138:**1**
organ, at Vassar College, 236:3
Oriskany, New York, battle of, 1777, 7

Warwick, New York, scene in, c.1875, 186–87:**2**
Washington, Fort (Fort Knyphausen), 56:**3**, 58–59:**1**
Washington, George:
 and "Empire" state, 7, 9, 85
 equestrian statue of, 156:**2**
 establishment of West Point, 88
 headquarters at Newburgh, 308:**2**
 house of, New York City, 110:**1** (at left)
 inauguration of, 1789, 70:**1**, 99
 land speculation, 7
 portrait of, 56:**1**
 in Revolutionary War, 7, 55, 56:**1**, 58–59, 61, 62, 64, 66, 308:**2**
watchbox, c.1800, 76:**1** (at right)
watches:
 advertisement for, 49:**3**
 store selling, 248–49:**3**
water, heating system for, 1844, 119:**4** (at bottom)
water cart, 77:**7**
waterfalls:
 in Catskill Mountains, 229:**3**
waterfalls:
 at Cohoes, 100–101:**2**
 Genesee Falls, 84:**1**, 94:**2**
 Niagara Falls, 254–55, 310:**1**
 New Croton Dam, 205:**5**
 at Watkins Glen, 310:**3**
water heater, 1844, 119:**4** (at bottom)
water power, 8, 254–55
water pumps:
 1768, 46–47:**2**
 c.1817, 75:**3**
 1844, 119:**4**
waters, mineral, 142–43:**1**
water supply, 118–19, 204–05
water tanks, on Ellis Island, 219:**5** (upper left)
Watervliet, New York, 190–91 (at right)
 map (as West Troy), 1871, xi
water wheel, of Burden Iron Works, 178–79:**3**
Watkins Glen, New York, waterfall at, 310:**3**
Waugh, Samuel, *The Battery* by, 146–47:**2**
weapons, *see* bows and arrows; cannon; rifles; spears; swords; tomahawks
weathervane, 76–77:**6**
Webb, Thomas, 47:**5**
Webster, Daniel, 9
Weed, Thurlow, 9
Weir, John F.:
 *Forging the Shaft* by, 168:**2**
 *The Gun Foundry* by, 169:**3**
 portrait of Sylvanus Thayer by, 89:**2**
Wells, H. G., on Niagara Falls, 255
wells, 75:**3** (right center), 114–15:**1** (at left), 182–83 (at right)
well sweep, 182–83 (at right)
Welsh immigrants, 147
Wesley's Chapel, New York City, 46–47:**3**
West, Benjamin, *Colonel Guy Johnson* by, 66:**2**
West, Benjamin, *Robert Fulton* by, c.1806, 98:**1**
Westchester County, New York, 5, 80, 266
 landscape, 204–05:**3**, 205:**4**
 views, 19c., 198–99

West India Company, 22
West Point, New York, 243
 military academy at, 88–89
 in Revolutionary War, 64:**1,2**
 steamboat *Clermont* passing, 98:**3**
 views of:
  1791, 88:**1**
  c.1812, 99:**4** (in background)
 and views of Hudson River, c.1830, 100:**1**, 101:**5**
West Point foundry, Cold Spring, New York, 168:**2**, 169:**3**
West Troy, *see* Watervliet
whale, 185:**6**
whale-oil lamps, 120:**1**
Wharton, Edith, photograph of, 263:**7**
wharves, 36–37:**1**, 86:**2**
 at Albany, 292:**1**
 at Buffalo, 192–93:**3**
 East River, c.1845, 168:**1** (at right)
 at Hoboken, New Jersey, 1940s, 284–85:**5**
 at New York City, 1870, xii-xiii (on map)
 steamboat (Whitehall St., New York City), 99:**5**
 unloading iron at, 297:**4**
wheat, *see* grain
wheat spikes, on Indian headdress, 40:**2**
wheels:
 for winding cable, 249:**4**
 water wheel, 178–79:**3**
wheelbarrows:
 1819, 75:**4**
 1870, 183–84
whistle, 33:**4**
Whiteface Mountain, view of, 311:**6**
White Plains, New York:
 battle map of, 1777, 59:**3**
 mansion in, 198–99:**3**
 view of, 1887, 198–99:**2**
Whitman, Walt, portraits of, 196:**2**, 262:**2**
Wightsboro, New York, dairy factory at, 184–85:**1**, 184:**2**
wigs:
 c.1730, 32–33:**5**
 1774, 55:**6**
Willard, Emma Hart, 191
Willard, Col. W. T., Civil War officer, 163:**4**
Willet, Margaret, 85:**3** (right figure)
Willet, Col. Marinus, 67:**5**
William and Mary, of England, 34
William Henry, Fort:
 plan of, 42:**1** (bottom)
 hotel near site of, 143:**4**
Williams, Edward, map of Virginia (detail) by, 1651, 23:**4**
Wilson, Malcolm, photograph of, 287:**8** (at right)
Wilson, Mrs. Malcolm, 287:**8**
windmills, 22–23:**1**, 187:**6**
wine production, 14, 185:**4,5**, 294–95:**4**
*Winter Landscape from Olana,* painting by F. E. Church, 241:**7**
Winthrop, John, library of, 52
Wolfe, Gen. James, 6
women, *see also* costume; portraits, women:
 education of, 134–35:**4**, 135:**5**, 191,

356